CW00956806

BLACK NIGHT OFF FINISTERRE

ARTHUR HAWKEY

BLACK NIGHT OFF FINISTERRE

*The Tragic Tale of an
Early British Ironclad*

Airlife
England

Copyright © 1999 Arthur Hawkey

First published in the UK in 1999
by Airlife Publishing Ltd

British Library Cataloguing-in-Publication Data
A catalogue record for this book
is available from the British Library

ISBN 1 84037 095 5

Typeset by Phoenix Typesetting, Ilkley, West Yorkshire
Printed in England by WBC Book Manufacturers, Bridgend, Glamorgan

Airlife Publishing Ltd
101 Longden Road, Shrewsbury, SY3 9EB, England

For R. and N. Philipson-Stow – good friends.

FOREWORD

THE STORY of HMS *Captain* and the fascinating decade of her creation came to my attention when I was in St Paul's Cathedral and noticed – as thousands had done before me – the two brass plaques which commemorate the loss of the *Captain*.

As I read the engraved finding of the court martial into the loss of the ship with its public and permanent condemnation of Press and Parliament – a unique indictment I believe – I decided to look further into the story.

As a result of my researches in the British Museum, Public Record Office, Royal United Services Institute*, Royal Institution of Naval Architects, National Maritime Museum, Imperial War Museum, and among old newspapers and magazines a story emerged of rivalry in Whitehall which, combined with pride and prejudice among public figures of the time, culminated in a great disaster at sea and a revolution in the design of warships.

I should like to thank the anonymous officials who helped me to find old documents, correspondence and photographs: I am also indebted to the Royal United Services Institute for permission to photograph the model of the hull of the *Captain* (now in the National Maritime Museum); and to officers of the British Shipbuilding Research Association for vetting the chapter on stability, the elementary nature of which is my responsibility.

Some of the most intriguing information came to me from the late Miss Kathleen Murray, of Palmiet River, Grabouw, Cape Province, South Africa, daughter of a Royal Navy ship's doctor, who disclosed to me what had previously been known only within her family, who had no knowledge of its significance: I am particularly grateful to Miss Murray. As will be seen, her disclosure alters history relating to the loss of HMS *Captain*.

I ask for tolerance from any professional sailors or naval architects who

* Formerly the Royal United Service Institution

may read this book for passages that may appear to them to be over-simplified. I have avoided technicalities as far as possible because this account of the *Captain* was not written primarily for experts, but for ordinary people whose knowledge of ships and the sea may be limited to that instinctive interest in them which is a pleasing characteristic of seafaring nations.

A.H.
Bickley,
Kent.

CONTENTS

CHAPTER 1

OF SHIPS AND SAILING MEN

The gale blew from the south west as the combined Channel and Mediterranean fleets, under the command of Admiral Sir Alexander Milne, buffeted their way to the north, Portsmouth bound with most sails furled and double reefs in those that dared the wind.

All ships lay over, mostly running free with the wind on the port quarter. From time to time they changed course towards the north west on the port tack to maintain ample distance between the ships and the lee shore of the Portuguese coast to the east. They sailed constantly heeled, yielding to the force of the gale; and occasionally they lurched still further as stronger squalls tore at the meagre, straining canvas and when a rogue wave heaved against the higher exposed hull on the windward side. The gale would become more westerly as the night wore on.

On such a night during the long wars against France, England's admirals could eye the weather vane in the Board Room of the Admiralty and know that the blockading English fleet was either sheltering in Torbay or standing off well into the Atlantic, confident that against such weather the French could not get out of their western ports. But now, in 1870, steam was well established to bring some independence of the wind's caprice; but not yet complete independence. In this fact lay the seeds of disaster.

The spray mingled with the slanting rain and lashed those of the crews unfortunate to be on watch in such weather. And it lashed a handful of men whose exposure to the storm was the luckiest thing that ever happened to them. For they were the only 18 survivors out of a crew of more than 500 who plunged to their deaths as they rested or slept when HMS *Captain*, newest, most controversial ship in the Royal Navy, turned over and sank in a few minutes on the night of 6–7 September 1870.

It was a deathroll greater than at Trafalgar; and it was more poignant since this was in peacetime and need not have happened if pride, prejudice and an ignorant clamour had not combined to override wiser counsel.

HMS *Captain* was an iron-hulled man-of-war built to test the ideas of Captain Cowper Phipps Coles, a naval officer and inventor who developed the system of putting ships' guns inside turrets, or armoured cylinders, which could be turned through a complete circle and, in theory, command the whole horizon.

This change in the method of mounting guns, a complete break with the centuries-old tradition of lining the guns in tiers along the sides of the ship, led ultimately to the development of the great naval vessels that came to maturity in two world wars this century, although Coles's precise method of gun mounting was improved and modified: but it was his idea.

This is the story of a momentous decade in the development of the Royal Navy; and one that reached its awful climax in a confused sea and gale off Cape Finisterre, on the Atlantic coast of Spain.

It is also the story of two men: one brilliant, inventive, impatient, persistent, who died with the ship he created – Captain Cowper Phipps Coles. The other: scientific, assertive, cautious, expert in his field, the civil servant trying to indicate the best road for naval science to take at a time when the fleets of the world were being reforged with new materials, new ideas; a time when gratuitous and not always sound advice abounded – Edward James Reed, Chief Constructor of the Navy.

To appreciate the feelings that were aroused by the long controversy of the 1860s as to whether guns mounted in rotatable turrets should displace the traditional method of mounting them along the ship's sides; or whether Reed's preference for grouping the guns together in a central armoured citadel (each gun firing to one side only, albeit with a traverse) should prevail, it must be appreciated that the turret alternative was the most revolutionary idea for centuries.

In more than 500 years since the first appearance of guns on ships during the reign of Edward III there had been only gradual development of shipbuilding in Britain. There were changes in rigging, in size, and the adaptation of the best features of Italian, Portuguese, Spanish and French ships which had all, in their turn, been superior in design to English vessels. But broadly, ships and their guns changed in detail and not conception.

Such was the conservatism and slow rate of progress that there was little difference between the *Caledonia*, mounting 120 guns and launched in 1810, and the *Royal Sovereign*, a three-decked ship-of-the-line that had been built nearly 200 years before, in 1637.

The two ships were of similar proportions and construction, had the same arrangement of decks and ports, and the *Caledonia*, the largest warship in Britain at her launching – and much later to become the Dreadnought hospital ship at Greenwich – represented only the latest variation in this centuries-old evolution.

To give but one example: naval officers had complained for many years about the structural weakness of their ships' sterns and their defencelessness aft, there being no gun ports cut in the stern. A heroic view might be that the Royal Navy had no need to be able to fire over its shoulder: but in unromantic practice it was a defect that went long unheeded.

There is an account of an action in 1794 between the frigate *Blanche* and the French frigate *La Pique*. The report says: "In the action the *Blanche*'s mizzenmast and, shortly afterwards, her mainmast were shot away. Just before this happened we had, with the intention of boarding, put up our helm to starboard and run across the stem of *La Pique*, her bowsprit coming over our quarter-deck.

"To secure her in this situation Captain Faulkner and myself made every rope on her that we could lay hold of fast round our capstan; and the end of the hawser being handed up, we effectually secured her by passing it also round her bowsprit.

"The *Blanche*'s main and mizzenmasts being shot away, and the head sails filling, she paid off before the wind, thus bringing *La Pique* astern, towing her by the bowsprit. We were immediately much annoyed from her quarter-deck guns, well served and pointing forwards, without our being able to return a gun, having no stern ports on the main deck. We had no alternative left but to blow out the stern frame.

"All the firemen with their buckets were assembled in the cabin and both the aft guns pointed against the stern frame. This made a clear breach on both sides and the fire was immediately extinguished. We now raked her with great effect, clearing her decks fore and aft, and they soon called out that they had surrendered."

This graphic but modest account says nothing of the resolution, quick thinking and opportunism that turned near defeat into victory in this desperate single-ship engagement. It is but one of many incidents in naval history when the quality of the ship's company made up for the defects in equipment.

But if Admiralty progress in shipbuilding design was slow, there was equally a lack of invention among private shipbuilders. The first recorded letters patent granted for improvements to ships are dated 17 January 1618. Between then and 1810 there was no really significant invention patented for ships except for the manufacture of hull sheathings and the construction of pumps – itself an indication of the leaky nature of the hulls. In fact, from 1618 to 1800 more than a third of the patents were for improvements in ships' pumps.

During the 18th century the stagnation in private shipbuilding was in large part due to a shipbuilding ring which had a monopoly in building large vessels. The East India Company, the largest buyer of ships, was forced to pay ridiculous prices to the Marine Interest, as the monopoly was called.

Whenever it was necessary to replace a worn-out or ship-wrecked vessel, the member of the Marine Interest which had built it claimed the right to build its successor. This custom, known as the 'hereditary bottom' system, continued until 1796.

If the East India Company had been able to ask for tenders in an open market there is little doubt that the competition among ship designers would have led to quicker advances in ship construction. As it was, shipbuilders were content to build much as they had always built. Good or bad, their ships were bound to be accepted; so there was no incentive to bold development.

During the early part of the 19th century there was progress in hull construction, and by the time Queen Victoria came to the throne the types of ships considered necessary for the Royal Navy were so well established that the Assistant Surveyor to the Royal Navy published a set of tables giving detailed information of the different classes of ships required for the navy of that day.

The arts of the shipwright, sawyer, blacksmith, joiner, millwright and caulker, with axe, adze, plane and iron forgings appeared to have reached their peak as far as naval vessels were concerned.

But the end of the wooden, sailing battleship was nigh. Typical of their passing was the *Goliath*, one of the last to be built. She was launched at Chatham in 1842 but she never sailed with the Fleet. She was put 'in ordinary'; that is to say she was moored in the Medway until it might be decided to complete her. She never did get her rigging and sails. For 15 years she lay in the Medway in the charge of shipkeepers – old sailors or marines who lived aboard as watchmen with their families.

In 1858 she was converted into a 60-gun screw ship: five years afterwards she was declared useless and again she was laid up in ordinary from 1863 to 1870. In 1870 she was lent to the managers of the Forest Gate school district; and in 1875, while serving as a schoolship in the Thames, she was destroyed by fire.

So ended the long era of the wooden walls of England; for iron had gone to sea – first as armour hung over wooden hulls, and then as the basic material for the hull itself. No longer need admirals like Collingwood, thinking of England's future, carry acorns in their pockets to plant on country walks lest oak for their great-grandchildren's ships should become scarce.

France led the way in 1859 with *La Gloire*, which had a 4-inch-thick band of armour all along the waterline and in front of the guns, firing in the traditional way through ports in the ship's sides.

It was obvious that Britain had to keep up with her neighbour and the government invited tenders for designs for a ship to match *La Gloire*. Fifteen designs were submitted from private shipbuilders and master shipbuilders of the royal dockyards. A design submitted by admiralty designers was accepted and resulted in the first British iron battleship, HMS *Warrior*.

But if iron had now displaced oak, steam had not yet superseded sail. It was still regarded as complementary to the full sailing rig of old. Owing to Britain's overseas commitments, it was still considered essential that an ocean-going warship should sail, so that her range would be unlimited and independent of the amount of coal in her bunkers, for the early steam engines were extravagant with fuel. The fact that the wind costs nothing was also an important consideration.

It was this policy that settled the fate of HMS *Captain*, for when she came to be built it led her designers to pursue this Admiralty requirement of world-wide sailing capability and to put tall masts and a full rig of sails and heavy spars on a hull that ought never to have been burdened with them.

CHAPTER 2

THE MAN WHO WAS RIGHT

Three revolutions were taking place in the navies of the world when E. J. Reed, Chief Constructor of the Navy, came into government service. Steam meant that a ship's speed and manoeuvrability no longer depended on extreme refinement of design, so as to get the slightest extra advantage from wind and wave; and it became instead rather dependent upon the power and cost of the engines installed.

The second great development was the explosive shell which was replacing the solid shot that had for centuries been the main iron missile in naval warfare.

Thirdly, ships were being plated with armour as a first step towards being built entirely of iron. As always, defence had to keep pace with attack – and vice versa – and so the thickness of armour, its consequent weight, and where it was to be applied, were questions of continuing controversy as naval men, and public opinion expressed in Press and Parliament, sought the best solution.

It was a novel problem and the answer was not easy to come by. A massive weight of iron cannot simply be applied to a ship where it may be most needed to keep out enemy fire without taking other things into consideration. The position of weight in a ship's hull and its effect on the sea-going qualities of the vessel are very important and must be carefully considered in any ship design.

Reed was constantly criticised by his detractors for not showing more enterprise in the ships he created. But as we look back on his work he is entitled to have it remembered that his was the great responsibility. The all-important guiding standard was that the Royal Navy should remain an effective fighting force wherever its world-wide duties might call it.

Criticism without responsibility is not difficult; nor does it have reper-cussions, as a rule. But when the Chief Constructor of the Navy built a ship, subject to Admiralty approval, it was there as enduring evidence of the quality of its builder's skill and judgment – or otherwise. Some of Reed's ships were not the best possible testimony to his professional ability; but he also had his successes and by the time he gave up office he had laid the foundation for the future development of battleships.

Some of his ships provoked acid comment from naval men but E. J. Reed was well able to look after himself in the field of controversy. He was a severe, forthright and articulate man; impatient of inexpert opinions and confident in the rightness of his own. At the height of the controversy between himself and Captain Coles, Reed said in a speech to the Greenwich Literary Institution in December 1863:

"On every side we are surrounded by inventive and critical persons; sometimes helpful, it is true, but much more often with useless projects of their own to urge; often with obvious or concealed interests to further; often with excellent objects in view, but without a spark of ability to guide them to their accomplishment. And remember:

'There is none we read of in torture's inventions,
Like a well-meaning fool with the best intentions.'

"The British Navy," said Reed, "is certainly a noble thing to labour for and it is an especially happy occupation to labour for it at a time like this when so many are ignorantly seeking to deprive it of some of its best and noblest features.

"When I think of our glorious past, of the accustomed pride and confidence with which we have, as a nation, lived and laboured and fought and conquered on the open ocean, and then turn to some of the abominable models upon which some would have us henceforth shape our fleets, I am astonished at the folly into which men allow themselves to be led.

"Remember where England is, anchored on the very edge of the stormiest ocean on the globe . . . the very first anxiety therefore of our men-of-war is seaworthiness, and I trust that the day is far distant when the people of England shall consent to see their navy dwarfed and frittered down into anything incompatible with supremacy on the sea. The mere power of keeping afloat will not sufficiently save us. Our home is on the deep and we must live there, not in half-sunk rafts, shut out from the light and air of heaven, but in spacious and healthy and comfortable ships, fit for our inhabitation in all oceans and climates."

To anyone interested in the subject all this was an undisguised attack on Captain Coles's proposals for sea-going ships with low sides to carry his invention of the turntable gun turret revolving in the main deck. Reed was clearly opposed to the concept and it was not necessary to mention names.

He was born at Sheerness on 20 September 1830 and first learnt about ships as a shipwright apprentice in the royal dockyard. At the age of 19 he was selected for the School of Mathematics and Naval Construction at Portsmouth. The school had been established only a year earlier and the principal was Dr Joseph Woolley, a distinguished Cambridge mathematician and one of the founders of the Institution of Naval Architects in later years.

Other students included Nathaniel Barnaby and F. K. Barnes who were afterwards to become closely associated with Reed in his work for the Admiralty. All three passed out from the school together in 1852. They were immensely enthusiastic about their work and the future it held out to them in those exciting days of changes at sea.

Reed was appointed supernumerary draughtsman at Sheerness dockyard and was attached to the mould loft. This was the department where the lines of the moulds, which determine the shape of a vessel's hull and its curve at any given point along its length, were worked out and drawn. Reed found his duties to be trivial and little more than routine. His vision of a brilliant future began to fade.

As an outlet for his creative energy and some sort of consolation for the lack of anything important or interesting in his work, Reed began to write poetry. Some of it was published in 1857. Under the title *Corona and Other Poems* it received flattering notices in the press.

This sort of sop to his frustrated shipbuilding ambition was only a passing relief. He had expected some responsible employment at Sheerness upon the details of design and construction of ships – the kind of work he had been trained for at Portsmouth.

Reed decided not to wait upon events in government employ and in 1853 accepted an offer to become editor of *The Mechanic's Magazine.* He held this job for several years but still occupied his spare time with ship design.

In 1854 he submitted to the Admiralty a design for a high-speed ironclad frigate, prepared in collaboration with Nathaniel Barnaby, who became Reed's brother-in-law. This design was not accepted but, at least, it brought him to the notice of the Admiralty.

A few uneventful years passed until the end of 1859, when Reed and Barnaby and other men trained in naval architecture were called together – with Dr Woolley, their headmaster at Portsmouth – and invited by John Scott Russell, a leading ship designer, to form an Institution of Naval Architects. Reed acted as honorary secretary during the period of preliminary organisation and was then elected permanent secretary of the Institution.

This was an important stage in his career. The formation of the Institution gave professional dignity and standing to the comparatively newly developed science of naval architecture – as distinct from the age-old *art* of shipbuilding – and the position of secretary identified Reed as a member of some importance.

From the Institution Reed submitted to the Admiralty a second plan for an ironclad ship. It was to be much smaller than his first proposal and the Admiralty were sufficiently impressed by it to retain Reed's services and to let him have the assistance of an Admiralty draughtsman.

From this collaboration designs were prepared in 1862 for the conversion of three wooden vessels – *Enterprise, Favourite* and *Research* – into ironclads which were to be protected by armour at the waterline and to have their main guns contained within a central armoured citadel. These designs were approved and work proceeded under Reed's control.

The employment of Reed as an extra-departmental designer was due to the impression he had made on the First Lord of the Admiralty, the Duke of Somerset. He saw great promise in the young naval architect, who brought a fresh mind and ideas to the somewhat unadventurous conventionalism of the Constructor's Department.

When, a few months later at the beginning of 1863, the Chief Constructor, Isaac Watts, retired, the Duke offered the position to Reed. In the circumstances Reed did not take up his new duties amid popular acclaim. On the contrary, many people saw in the appointment of a man of 33, with no shipbuilding successes behind him yet, a gross error of judgment. He was considered to be far too young for a post carrying with it such far-reaching consequences for the security of the nation.

Sir Frederick Smith, MP for Chatham, criticised the appointment in the House of Commons, saying that Reed was not properly qualified, had been only "an apprentice" and had "never built a ship."

Reed, who heard this speech from his place on the officials' benches, wrote to Sir Frederick complaining forcefully of his inaccurate remarks and personal abuse "in a place where I have no opportunity of answering you."

Sir Frederick Smith reported this letter to the Speaker, as a breach of parliamentary privilege, and Reed was called to the Bar of the House to apologise for his action.

"I am quite confident that I wrote that letter under great irritation," he said, making the formal abject apology that the House of Commons expects on such occasions: and there the matter ended.

It was, however, an early indication that E. J. Reed was not a man to take criticism with a smile, or hold back from stating his own case. His experience at the Bar of the House, which supplicants there usually find somewhat awesome, did not prevent his returning to his own defence a few months later in a speech at Greenwich, where he lived.

19

"Some extremely penetrating and pure-minded people have discovered in a recent appointment of mine a most disgraceful 'job'", he said. "I suppose it does seem disgraceful to some people for the Board of Admiralty to appoint to an office involving much hard work and much grappling with difficult and pressing problems, any man who has neither attained the age of 60, nor taken part at elections in what are called 'Government Boroughs.' But the class of people who think in this fashion is not numerous now, and ere long it will doubtless become altogether extinct." No doubt Sir Frederick Smith, if he read the speech, recognised himself.

Reed was Chief Constructor from 1863 to 1870. It was a critical time, for the early ironclads – *Warrior, Minotaur* and other types built under the previous regime – were not entirely satisfactory, and many proposals for radical changes in future designs were being canvassed.

The most popular proposal – because it caught the imagination of many influential people and also that of the press – was Captain Coles's idea. It was the public support for the notion of a sea-going turret ship – as well as the facility with words of both Reed and Coles – that made them public antagonists in the popular, free-for-all debate on which way ship design should develop.

Reed's particular and onerous task was to determine the line of development for the Navy's new ships without, on the one hand, being trammelled by tradition nor, on the other, being tempted to follow unscientific suggestions from influential quarters which, though they might appear to be bravely revolutionary and convincing to a layman, were, to the professional ship designer, unsound.

Reed's difficulty, among others, was that of presenting a convincing and generally understood answer to these pressure groups; for it must be remembered that great advances in the theory of nautical design had been made comparatively recently. Theories, based on mathematical equations, were incomprehensible to the layman; and even experts disagreed about things which are accepted as basic principles today.

Reed might be sure in his own mind, from his own scientific understanding, that a ship of a certain design was likely to prove to be unseaworthy, or even dangerous, but there was not yet a common acceptance of new-found theories that would, today, make his reasoning irrefutable – at any rate among professionals.

Part of the trouble was the lack of easy communication. It is impossible to explain a complicated subject unless the language of expression is commonly understood. The extent of the poor understanding of ship design, even among senior naval officers, became clear at the court martial on the survivors from HMS *Captain.*

Reed was Chief Constructor until 7 July 1870, when he resigned to join Whitworth's of Manchester. It was a year of mixed fortune professionally, for Reed. The long controversy with Captain Coles seemed to have come to an end with a triumph for the naval officer, whose wonder vessel, the *Captain*, was afloat and apparently, after two successful cruises, a ship that seemed to justify the inventor's dogged persistence and to condemn Reed's years of opposition to the design.

It had been, nevertheless, a year of official recognition for Reed. The Admiralty had approved, in February 1870, an increase in his salary to £1500 a year; and after some months delay, finally ordered, in June, payment of a £5000 award (recommended in February) in appreciation of the improvements in shipbuilding methods brought about by the Chief Constructor.

But whatever improvements or technical advances Reed may have been responsible for, these were things of which the general public were not so fully aware, and thus did nothing to mitigate the popular image of him as an incompetent, unimaginative civil servant.

It was Reed, assisted by his former student friends, Barnaby and Barnes, and others whom he gathered around him in the Admiralty service, who invented a method of ship construction called the longitudinal and bracket frame system which became the standard method of building all iron battleships right through to the 20th century. It was a big advance in hull construction for iron vessels over the traditional wooden shipbuilding practice which had at first been followed.

The system was laid down by Reed for the *Bellerophon*, the first battleship that he built soon after taking office as Chief Constructor. The *Bellerophon* was a great step forward in design on the previous ironclads of the *Warrior* class. They had been very long ships, not easily manoeuvrable, and with all their guns along the broadside in the traditional manner. Reed's general aim was to produce shorter ships that were more handy, and to develop their end-on fire without sacrificing the weight of broadside they could deliver.

The *Bellerophon*, launched in May 1865, was a high-sided ship, fully rigged in addition to her engines, and she was protected by a belt of iron at her waterline. Her heavy guns were grouped amidships in an armoured citadel which also covered the vital parts of the ship.

Reed attempted to give her end-on fire by mounting a smaller battery behind armour in the bows. But excessive weight on the bows of a ship affects its behaviour at sea, and in later designs he improved on this by introducing recessed gun ports at the corners of the central citadel.

But to Captain Coles and his many admirers this was only tinkering with the problem of gaining maximum fire power in all directions. "Turn the gun round, not the ship", was Coles's tireless theme; and, of course, there was a lot to be said for it. But in his opinion it also involved the ship having a low side with the guns firing clear across the main deck; and no gunports along the side to let in the enemy's shot and shell.

This was a design that Reed would only accept for coastal defence where it was unnecessary to spend long periods at sea or endure without shelter any kind of bad weather. The monitor design, as it was called, were small ships of low freeboard, and without sail, which could not cruise long distances since they were limited in range to the amount of coal they could carry and, in any case, were not designed to be lived in at sea for long periods. They were virtually floating batteries and were extremely valuable in coast and port defence.

Reed, however, would not consider putting sails on such vessels. This was the point of great divergence between Coles and Reed. Coles, a professional sailor, insisted that big cruisers – virtually large monitors but carrying a full rig of sails – could be built to carry his turntable turrets anywhere in the world; and fire in any direction, no matter where the ship was headed.

Before disaster proved Reed right in resisting this theory, he laid down in November 1869 – nearly a year before the *Captain* sank, and while she was still building – the *Devastation*, a large sea-going monitor entirely without masts: she had Coles's turrets mounted forward and aft of a central superstructure, and no forecastle or poop to interfere with their fire. This same characteristic of gun siting is seen in men-of-war of this century: only the size and efficiency of the guns and the design of the turrets have changed.

The *Devastation* was not finished until after Reed left the Admiralty, and he complained that she was modified in several important details from his design. But nevertheless, she may be regarded as the forerunner of the long line of battleships that played such significant roles in two world wars.

The measure of Reed is given – as accurately as the circumstances of the time permitted – in a *Times* leading article written when he left the Admiralty service after a long-standing disagreement with the First Lord over the building of more *Captain* class ships before the first one had been fairly tried.

The Times said: "He has been far in advance of the naval advisers to the Admiralty in all matters connected with naval ordnance. It is owing to him that the guns of 9-inch, 10-inch and 11-inch calibre, with which our latest ships are armed, have been mounted in these vessels, and we believe it is no secret that one reason of his readiness to be lured from the public service has been the opposition he has encountered in still further developing and improving the ordnance of our ships of war.

"If, in so difficult a struggle, he has at times been impatient of opposition, intolerant of criticism, jealous of rivalry, or even too much inclined to self-assertion, great allowance should be made for the position in which he was placed, and the natural feelings of a strong character. Mr Reed has often been wrong. In his heated advocacy of broadsides against turrets and his depreciation of low freeboard for sea-going cruisers, he has manifested too strongly for the public interest a personal antagonism to Captain Coles; and time has pronounced upon these two questions in favour of Captain Coles, and adversely to Mr Reed."

But, of course, when *The Times* leader writer paid this qualified tribute to Reed HMS *Captain* was still afloat – an apparent triumphant vindication of Captain Coles's theories.

Time would indeed pronounce upon the question; but on the next occasion, when it would reverse its opinion, it would be with the full knowledge and understanding of all the grim facts.

CHAPTER 3

THE MAN WHO WAS WRONG

Cowper Phipps Coles, the man most identified with the *Captain*, was born at Ditcham Park, Hampshire in 1819, the third son of the Reverend John Coles. He went straight into the Navy from school and passed his examination for commissioned rank in 1838.

His service followed a fairly normal course. He was promoted to Lieutenant in January 1846 and the first significant step in his career came in October 1853, when he was chosen by Rear-Admiral Sir Edmund Lyons as his Flag Lieutenant aboard HMS *Agamemnon*, in which he served during the Crimean War.

Coles was also with the fleet during the attack on Russian forts at Sebastopol on 17 October 1854. A deep impression was made on him by the comparative helplessness of an enormous fleet of wooden ships against the fire of the shore batteries.

The fleet was mauled and never again attempted a mass onslaught against well-sited shore guns. The hopelessness of getting to grips with the enemy in such a situation – although not an unfamiliar one in naval warfare – started his mind pondering an alternative way of bringing heavy ships' guns close inshore without having them mounted in cumbersome three-deck battleships, unable to navigate shallow waters.

Coles was promoted commander on 13 November and, a few months later, was given command of the paddle steamer *Stromboli*, operating in the Black Sea. While in *Stromboli*, and faced again with the difficulty of operating in shallow waters, Coles conceived the idea of building a raft which could carry a 32-pounder gun and be floated close inshore.

The raft, called *Lady Nancy*, was made in a single night from 29 casks cradled in a framework of spars and, when finished, it was 45 feet long by 15 feet broad. Part of it was decked over with planks.

A press correspondent described its building:

"Seldom has a more lively scene, or a more perfect display of energy been witnessed than that which presented itself on the quarter-deck of the *Stromboli* during the building of the *Lady Nancy*. The ever-being-swept,

24

dazzling white parade ground was now a building yard. All hands saw not only the importance, but the necessity of the work, and in the incredibly short space of 12 hours had provided themselves with a gun-boat which, when carrying a long 32-pounder gun weighing 42 cwt, 100 rounds of ammunition, a 7-inch hawser and 18 men, drew only 20 inches of water."

Coles, of course, was the driving force behind this work, devising, improvising, as the job proceeded. Next day the *Stromboli* towed the *Lady Nancy* 100 miles in a rough sea to Taganrog, in the Sea of Azoff, floated it in through shoal waters and destroyed a large quantity of Russian stores; an exploit that was applauded with great enthusiasm in England.

Encouraged by this success, Coles improved on the design and made a raft, supported by empty casks, to carry a 95-cwt gun complete with a hemispherical iron shield. When in action the raft could be submerged partly by filling some of the casks with water. In this state the raft was also virtually fireproof if hit by hot shot or shell; and owing to the large number of separate casks used in its construction it was almost unsinkable.

Coles claimed: "If a 13-inch shell should strike such a raft it would do little damage beyond destroying one or two casks, the loss of whose buoyancy could well be spared."

His idea was to build a number of these rafts, which were to be 90 feet × 30 feet, and take them in sections to the Baltic to attack the Russian forts at Kronstadt, which had hitherto proved impregnable to the British ships. Each raft drew only 3 feet 7 inches of water fully loaded with its gun, and it could be further immersed to 5 feet 3 inches, still leaving the gun 4 feet 6 inches clear of the sea.

He also suggested that some of the rafts should be steam powered so that they could tow the rest. They were then to make their way along the shallow waters towards the forts, which were not designed to be able to fire on such 'un-navigable' waters.

Rear-Admiral Sir Edmund Lyons was impressed by this invention of his former Flag Lieutenant and appointed a committee to investigate it on the spot. It consisted of Rear-Admiral Sir Houston Stewart, Captain Arthur Cumming, Captain E. A. Inglefield, Mr Rumble, Chief Engineer of HMS *Royal Albert*, and the carpenter of HMS *Hannibal.*

They visited *Stromboli* and examined Coles's models with great interest. They reported enthusiastically to Sir Edmund Lyons and, in pointing out the advantages of the raft, said: "Looking to the probable nature of future operations against our present enemy (Russia), we are of opinion that this proposal merits the immediate attention of Her Majesty's Government and, in order that the full benefit may be derived from it, we venture to think it desirable that Commander Coles should be directed to proceed to England and personally to explain his proposals to their Lordships.

"We further suggest that under present circumstances *secrecy* is desirable."

Lyons agreed and ordered Coles home in November 1855 to outline his plan to the Admiralty. Coles was instructed to superintend the building of a number of rafts to his design, but before they could be completed the war ended and, in common with many other officers, Coles soon found himself with no employment and on half-pay.

Any interest that there had been at the Admiralty in his idea faded at the coming of peace. The model of Coles's raft, which was actually pointed at both ends and was equipped with armoured prow and rudder mechanism, finally found a home as a naval curiosity in the Royal United Services Institute in Whitehall, London, of which Coles was a member.

The proposed raft, which Coles referred to in later years as "a vessel" when he was disputing whether he or the American, Ericsson, had first invented this kind of gun-boat, carried its gun in a hemispherical shield.

Coles did not at that time consider making the gun and shield revolve, since his vessel was designed to attack stationary forts in the Baltic and Black Sea, and it could have been turned quickly enough to make the added expense and complication of a turntable unnecessary.

Coles said: "I soon found out how useless it was for me to argue against prejudice and theory, and how hopeless it was to try and introduce into the Navy a novel invention, the offspring of practical observation in actual warfare. And so it was that I and many others were doomed to witness hundreds of guns and thousands of the finest seamen that ever trod a deck rendered useless in the attack on an enemy's fortress."

So many objections were raised to his plans in his peacetime nego-tiations with the Admiralty that Coles asked the advice of Isambard Brunel, the Victorian engineer and designer of, among other famous ships, the *Great Western*, which began the first regular steamship service across the Atlantic.

Brunel, after thoroughly considering Coles's proposals, complimented him on them and assured him that he had "the right idea." He went so far as to say that he had been devising a vessel for the same kind of warfare – close inshore attack – but that Coles's idea was so much better than his own that he would "think no more about it."

When Coles asked what his fee was for the advice, the great engineer replied: "Nothing: it is my pleasure to help a naval officer who is trying to benefit his country." His parting words to Coles were: "Go on, perse-vere, and you will succeed," words which Coles later said "often cheered me under the greatest discouragements."

This was 1856, some six years before the American *Monitor* was to startle the navies of the world during the American Civil War.

By March 1859 Coles had developed his ideas for his shielded guns by proposing that they would be fitted with turntables and be installed in larger vessels; he suggested that they could also be used in forts. He received encouragement from *The Times*, but little from the Admiralty.

Happening to be in Portsmouth about this time, Coles showed his latest plans to Rear-Admiral the Hon. George Grey, Superintendent of the Royal Dockyard, who was so struck by their feasibility that he brought them to the notice of the Prince Consort.

Coles was summoned to Osborne, the royal home in the Isle of Wight, and explained his ideas to the Prince. Five times more Albert sent for him and went into the invention with the greatest detail until he appeared to understand it thoroughly. Coles was full of hope that this royal interest might lead to some influence being brought to bear on his behalf at the Admiralty.

Coles's idea at this time was for a ship of 9200 tons with no less than eight revolving turrets in line along the centre of the main deck with a further two, side by side, up forward, to sweep the areas on each side and forward of the foremast.

In submitting his sketch for this revolutionary vessel Coles did not show where the ship's rigging would be. The Controller of the Navy pointed out that the rigging would interfere with the fire of several guns and that either the number of turrets would have to be reduced or the ship would have to be made much larger so that by spacing out masts and turrets more this difficulty might be overcome. At this time, of course, Reed was not yet in the Constructor's department.

As a first step towards testing Coles's invention the Admiralty agreed to finance the building of an experimental turret. It was commenced in 1859 but progress on it was very slow and it was not finally completed for two years.

Meanwhile, public interest in Coles's invention increased and Prince Albert urged the Duke of Somerset to build a turret ship at once, although he agreed "it would not be prudent to restrict ourselves to vessels of this novel construction; but we should give the country the benefit of possessing some such. Should Captain Coles's plan succeed, his ships will be vastly superior to those we are now building."

The Coles turret was completed in 1861 and mounted in the floating battery, *Trusty*. It came triumphantly through exacting trials at Shoeburyness: it was described by the officer conducting the trials as "one of the most formidable inventions adapted to naval warfare, as well as coast defences that has ever come to my notice."

The turret, after being hit 33 times with 68-lb, 40-lb and 100-lb projectiles, was still in perfect working order and virtually undamaged.

As a result of these experiments the Admiralty decided to go ahead with the building of a mastless ironclad armed with the turrets, to be used in coast defence. The ship was to be the *Prince Albert*, of 3880 tons, armed with four turrets; but the Queen's husband, who died on 14 December 1861, did not live to see Britain's first iron turret ship which he had advocated so strongly.

The *Prince Albert* was commenced in April 1862 and was completed in February 1866. She remained on the Navy List for 33 years, the second longest life of any British capital ship.

But gratifying and remunerative though it was to Coles that his invention was being taken up, the building of a coast defence ship with a maximum range of seven days economical steaming was somewhat far removed from his basic idea of a sea-going cruiser.

His dream was of an invincible navy, economically armed with his invention. He argued that two pairs of large guns in turrets could throw just as heavy weight of metal as a greater number of smaller guns mounted on the broadside principle: and since with Coles's system the metal would be thrown in very large pieces it was bound to do more damage to an enemy.

Although the Admiralty had conceded this and the other advantages of the turret for coast defence vessels – and the *Prince Albert* was under construction – they were yet to be convinced of the advantages of turrets in a fully-rigged capital ship.

In 1861 HMS *Warrior* was the first of the iron-built armoured warships. She was 6109 tons, 380 feet long, 58 feet wide and carried a crew of 705 men. She was fully equipped as a sailing ship and, in fact, had graceful clipper-style bows. Her steam-driven screw could be lifted out of the water when she was under sail. In her old age she served as an accommodation hulk at Portsmouth under the name *Vernon III*, and she was sold for breaking in 1924.

But at the time when Coles was trying to impress his views on the Admiralty, *Warrior* represented a powerful example of ship design in the era of naval construction before E. J. Reed's appointment.

And so, in 1861, Captain Coles could be found writing to the Admiralty from his home in Hyde Vale, Greenwich, stating that he could build a ship "not more than 320 feet long, about 48 feet beam, 23 feet draught of water, 5600 tons displacement and carry a broadside of at least 16 100-pounders under cupolas. This vessel shall be equal to the *Warrior* in speed, fighting powers, number of days' fuel and sea-going qualities, and should cost at least £100,000 less."

He pointed out that his ship, being shorter and not so deep in the water, would be more manoeuvrable than the long *Warrior* and more economical to run.

But their Lordships in Whitehall were not yet ready to authorize anything so expensive as an experimental ship of this kind: and they wrote and told Coles so.

Captain Cowper Phipps Coles, of course, took up his pen again.

CHAPTER 4

DUEL OF THE "IRON MONSTERS"

Meanwhile, on the other side of the Atlantic, where the American Civil War was showing no sign of an early end, events were taking shape that were to be of great value to Coles in his struggle with the Admiralty; for a vessel akin to his own conception of a man-of-war was to prove itself in actual combat.

On 17 April 1861, the State of Virginia seceded from the Union and joined the Southern rebels. The commandant of the United States Navy Yard at Norfolk, Virginia, scuttled four ships to prevent their falling into the hands of the rebels; shells were thrown into the river but an attempt to destroy the dry dock failed.

Destruction of stores was bungled and the Southern States therefore found themselves in possession of a valuable naval yard, over 1000 guns, shells (which they recovered from the river where they had been dumped), and thousands of barrels of powder. But their most important gain at Norfolk was the United States warship, *Merrimac*, which they raised from the harbour bed, cut down to the berth deck and remodelled as an ironclad. Work began on the ship on 11 July 1861.

When completed, the *Merrimac* looked like the roof of a house floating on the water. Both ends of the vessel's deck were covered with protective plating for 70 feet and, when the ship was in fighting trim, were just awash. The midship section, 170 feet long, formed a roof-like citadel of heavily armoured decks rising from either side of the ship at an angle of 35 degrees.

The 'roof' was built of pitch pine and oak 24 inches thick and covered by 4 inches of iron plating. Three heavy guns glared out from behind this shield on each side; and there were two light guns on bow and stern, making 10 in all.

A great cast iron-beak was bolted on to the bows, making a formidable ram. Steam driven, and originally a ship of 3500 tons mounting 40 guns in the old broadside style, she emerged from the dock in the spring of

1862, a grotesque monster like no other fighting ship that anyone had ever seen before.

News of her building had soon reached the United States Navy Department in Washington and the danger of having no vessel to stand up to her was immediately realized. The US Navy was blockading 3000 miles of coast and although the rebels frequently dodged through, there had been no serious challenge to it from the South, who had only limited facilities for ship building until the Norfolk yard fell into their hands.

The US Navy's solution was readily to hand in the form of John Ericsson, Swedish-born engineer and inventor, who had as early as 1846 conceived a 1200-ton iron vessel of revolutionary design which had been favourably considered by Napoleon III, to whom Ericsson had offered it during the Crimean War. But that war ended before Ericsson's ship could be built. Now it was to have its second chance, far-reaching in its effect on the navies of the world.

Ericsson described his ship to a sceptical American Navy Board. The ship, which was virtually submerged apart from its turtle-back iron deck, had two 11-inch guns mounted in a cylindrical armoured turret which could be turned by steam engines through a complete circle. Only the turret and pilot house stood up from the curved iron deck. Not the least important aspect of the new design was that its inventor guaranteed to build the ship in 90 days. It was October 1861 and, with the *Merrimac* already four months a'building, there was no time to be lost.

Ericsson accomplished one of the most amazing feats in the history of ship building. He superintended the construction of his 'floating battery', working from early morning until far into the night, drawing plans, improvising, designing, inventing as he went. He was literally a one-man design team. More than 40 patentable ideas were embodied in the vessel. All the time the Naval Department were urging, criticising and threatening non-payment if the ship were not completed in the time promised. It was. She was launched on 30 January 1862 and was turned over to the Navy on 19 February.

She was named the *Monitor* and the word has since been used to describe all vessels which follow her general principles of design and use. The idea for the name was Ericsson's own. He proposed it in a letter to the Assistant Secretary of the Navy in January 1862: "The impregnable and aggressive character of this structure will admonish the leaders of the Southern rebellion that the batteries on the banks of their rivers will no longer present barriers to the entrance of the Union forces. The iron-clad intruder will thus prove a severe monitor to those leaders. But there are other leaders who will also be startled and admonished by the booming guns of the impregnable iron turret. Downing Street will hardly view with indifference this last 'Yankee notion', this monitor. To the Lords of the Admiralty the new craft will be a monitor, suggesting doubts as to the propriety of completing those four steel-clad ships at three and a half million apiece. On these and many other similar grounds, I propose to name the new battery *Monitor*."

The *Monitor* was little more than half the length of the *Merrimac*, and her displacement was only 987 tons compared with the *Merrimac*'s 3000 odd. Ericsson's ship was in two sections: the hull, completely submerged, was 124 feet long, 18 feet wide at its flat bottom and 34 feet wide at the top, where it joined the main section – the raft-like, wood and armour-plated deck which was of similar plan outline to the hull but longer and wider, so that it overlapped it all round. The general appearance of the *Monitor* was like an elongated shallow metal pan comprising the hull, with a heavy iron-bound lid of the same shape, but considerably longer and somewhat wider laid on top of it, ie the deck. Ericsson described his invention as a fort on a raft. It was not pretty, nor ship-shape according to mid-nineteenth-century ideas, but it was the germ of the modern battleship.

When afloat the *Monitor* looked something like a submarine coming to the surface, and a moderate sea would wash freely over its deck. Ericsson got the idea from his boyhood memories of rafts on the lakes of Sweden. He recalled: "The raftsman in his cabin experiences very little motion, the seas breaking over his nearly submerged craft; these seas at the same time worked the sailing vessels nearly on their beam ends."

It was a curious coincidence that Captain Coles designed his first shielded gun to fire from a raft. There was some doubt as to which of the two men first conceived the idea for the turret. They worked independently but may eventually have profited by each other's experience. Coles certainly demonstrated the value of the protected gun on a low floating base during the Crimean War, but it was left to the Americans to demonstrate to the world in actual warfare that the Iron Age had come to stay at sea.

Although disaster came to the *Monitor* later through certain aspects of her design, Ericsson did not allow the fault that destroyed the *Captain* to be built into his ship – although the contract called for it.

He was required by the Navy Department to "furnish masts, spars, sails and rigging of sufficient dimensions to drive the vessel at the rate of six knots per hour in a fair breeze of wind." But Ericsson had ideas of his own about stability in vessels of shallow draught when fitted with masts and sails, and he ignored this part of the contract. It does not appear that any naval officer attempted to enforce this requirement, and so the *Monitor* took to sea as a steamer with only her turret and pilot house appearing above deck level.

She had no funnel. Smoke from the fires of her two boilers, which occupied practically the whole of the height of the submerged hull, escaped through a short flue to a grated hole in the deck. This was so that nothing should obstruct the fire of the guns. As there were no air downtakes or ventilators, a mild forced draught ventilating system was provided. Two steam engines drove two large fans which sucked air in through gratings in the deck, similar to those provided for the smoke to escape, and blew it into the engine and stoke holds where it had no way out except through the furnaces.

Low iron coamings, or splash barriers, surrounded these various deck gratings, intended to prevent water getting in during rough weather, but when cleared for action they were removed, leaving the deck entirely clear except for the pilot house.

On 19 February, three weeks after launching, the *Monitor* had a trial trip that was such a failure that she had to be towed home. It seemed that conservative naval men who had predicted she would never last to fire her guns might be proved right. But the faults were not surprising considering the speed with which she had been built – by a number of different contractors – from rough, hurriedly drawn plans.

The main engines broke down through a faulty valve seating but this was easily remedied. The gun mounts were damaged because they were fired without the recoil mechanism being engaged; but the damage was only slight.

The rudder also would not work but when the naval authorities proposed to take the *Monitor* into dry dock and fit a new rudder, Ericsson, whose pride in his invention was formidable, cried out: "The *Monitor* is mine and I say it shall not be done." He was a man of powerful voice and personality and he went on in contemptuous tones: "Put in a new rudder! They would waste a month doing that; I will make her steer just as easily in three days."

Like Coles, he had little time for the official mind but, unlike Coles, his impatient collaboration with the Navy came at a time of great urgency and he was able to enforce his will – which was preferable to argument and delay.

For the *Merrimac* (renamed the *Virginia*) was abroad. She was first sighted at noon on 8 March 1862 by the frigate, USS *Cumberland*, on patrol off Sewell's Point at the mouth of the Elizabeth River. The strange ship, escorted by two small gunboats, slipped easily downstream and ignored the opening fire from the *Cumberland*. She simply increased speed and headed straight for the wooden ship which dared to bar her progress to the sea.

The *Merrimac's* iron ram ripped into the *Cumberland's* side and she shuddered under the blow. At the same time the *Merrimac* opened fire. She withdrew, leaving a great hole in the *Cumberland's* side and the two vessels continued firing at each other at close range.

The engagement lasted until 3.35 p.m., the *Cumberland* gradually settling throughout until the water had risen to the main hatchway, virtually filling her hull; then she listed to port as her gunners, bare-footed and stripped to the waist, gave a parting shot and jumped overboard to swim ashore as the *Cumberland* disappeared with colours still flying.

After sinking the *Cumberland* the *Merrimac,* uninjured except for the loss of her iron ram which she had left embedded in the *Cumberland's* side, turned towards a second United States ship, the *Congress,* which had been engaged by the smaller gunboats accompanying the *Merrimac.*

Having seen what the "ugly monster" – as one report called it – had done to the *Cumberland,* the captain of the *Congress* ran his ship ashore so as to save her from complete loss. The *Merrimac* placed herself astern of the *Congress* and raked her from a range of 150 yards with her broadside. The *Congress* had only two stern guns with which to reply and was also being fired upon by the smaller gunboats to starboard. Her stern guns were soon disabled and, being then unable to bring a single gun to bear upon the *Merrimac,* the *Congress* hauled down her colours.

Before this final act of surrender the ship had been on fire in various places almost from the beginning of the action; she continued to burn until 2 a.m. the next morning. Of the *Cumberland's* crew of 376, 121 were killed and casualties aboard the *Congress* totalled 120.

Losses among the Southern ships were but two killed and eight wounded; and the *Merrimac* withdrew for the night, her only damage, after engaging ships of 24 guns and 50 guns, being the loss of her stanchions and iron railings, broken muzzles on two guns and the loss of her 1500-lb cast-iron beak.

A third United States ship, the steam frigate *Minnesota,* had run aground early in the day and had taken no effective part in the action. Owing to the state of the tide, the *Merrimac* could get no nearer than a mile from the stranded frigate that evening and withdrew, expecting to finish her off in the deeper water next day.

While this destruction was being wrought the *Monitor,* her defects repaired, was plunging porpoise-like south from New York, which she had left on the afternoon of 6 March, the day before the *Merrimac* appeared.

It was a very rough passage. Seas broke over the coamings round the deck gratings and water cascaded into the engine-room, nearly putting out the fires and stopping the pumps for four hours at one period through lack of steam.

She came near to foundering at this time from water that also got into the vessel under the base of the turret and through the anchor-cable ports at her bows. The blowers stopped because the driving belts got wet and the engine and stokeholds, which filled with suffocating gases from the fires, had to be abandoned. The engineers were dragged out, apparently dead, but they revived when laid on top of the turret beyond the reach of the sea.

The *Monitor* was kept afloat by means of hand pumps until the storm passed and her crew regained control in smoother water. It was an epic beginning to an historic encounter. At 4 p.m. on 8 March those on board the *Monitor* heard the sound of guns; but it was night before the little iron gunboat, guided by the light of the burning *Congress*, anchored near the stranded *Minnesota* and heard the news of the *Merrimac*'s onslaught.

At dawn the next day, a Sunday, the *Merrimac* moved in towards the *Minnesota* again. Now it was the turn of the *Merrimac*'s crew to experience something of a surprise such as their own appearance had caused among the Northern ships. They too, saw a craft like nothing they had ever seen before. "An immense shingle floating on the water, with a gigantic cheese box rising from its centre; no sails, no wheels, no smokestacks, no guns," an officer of the *Merrimac* recalled. This last observation, as they were soon to learn, could not have been more mistaken.

At 6 a.m. the lookouts on the *Minnesota* reported that the *Merrimac* was in sight. As she closed in the stranded *Minnesota* opened fire with her stern guns. The *Merrimac* was holding her course, her broadside ready, when the little *Monitor* suddenly steamed out from behind the *Minnesota* and placed herself between the two adversaries, virtually alongside the *Merrimac*. So far as size went it was a David against a Goliath. During the course of this manoeuvre the *Merrimac* had continued firing at the *Minnesota* with only an occasional blast at the strange little vessel.

When the ships were level with each other on parallel but opposite courses, the *Merrimac* gave her a full broadside. The shock was stupendous but when the crew of the *Monitor* realized that their turret continued to turn and that the shots had not penetrated, grimy grins were exchanged and they worked their guns eagerly.

Both ships stood up to the pounding. The *Monitor*'s shots ripped up the iron plates of the *Merrimac* but her armour was not pierced. Her own fire only stunned or startled the *Monitor*'s gunners from its crashing impact against the turret.

The *Monitor* tried to ram the *Merrimac*'s propeller as she crossed her stern but missed it by about two feet. The *Monitor* manoeuvred better than her big opponent and although many broadsides were aimed at her as she darted about, her lowness in the water caused many of the shots to fly harmlessly overhead. Those that struck her turret and pilot house glanced off, leaving only slight dents.

The position of the pilot house prevented full use being made of the revolving gun housing, since to fire ahead within the few degrees of the *Monitor*'s bow would have endangered those in the pilot house.

Neither could full advantage of this new type of gunnery be taken in this engagement. Observation was difficult from inside the turret and messages had to be carried by word of mouth between the pilot house and the turret to let the gunners know how their aim was.

The *Merrimac* also tried ramming and after manoeuvring for an hour did manage to catch the *Monitor* at a disadvantage; but a last-minute change of direction by the turret ship caused the blow to be a glancing one and it did no damage. At the moment of impact the *Monitor* fired a solid shot squarely in the forward part of the *Merrimac*'s gun armour. It shook the vessel through and through but, because the charge of powder was limited to 15 pounds in the *Monitor* owing to the experimental nature of her gun mounting, the shot did not penetrate even at zero range.

The two ships blazed away at each other until nearly noon and finally the *Merrimac* withdrew and the *Minnesota* was saved. Honours were about even. Both ships could still manoeuvre; neither was seriously damaged. In fact, it was the *Monitor* that withdrew first. A shell that struck the pilot house seriously wounded her captain and dislodged the plate forming the top of the pilot house. It was decided to withdraw to repair this; and the opportunity was also taken in the lull to get up ammunition.

The *Merrimac* took no advantage of the *Monitor*'s withdrawal, except to disengage herself and steam towards Norfolk, whence she came. She was still within range when the *Monitor*, her plate replaced, returned to the action; but the *Merrimac* held her course for Norfolk and did not return fire.

The *Merrimac* was found to have been struck 97 times during her two-day engagement. Twenty of these dents in her armour were from the *Monitor*'s guns.

During the fight the *Monitor* fired 41 shots, roughly one every six minutes. If this does not seem to be a rapid rate of fire, it should be remembered that apart from the difficulty of handling a completely novel type of ship and gun arrangement, it was in the days when guns still had to be served mainly by hand; be swabbed out after each firing to remove any glowing embers that might prematurely set off the next charge, have the charge rammed down the muzzle, have the shot pushed down after it, the fuse inserted, the gun manhandled back to the firing point, aim – and fire.

In the *Monitor*'s turret there were also huge iron pendulums which swung down to screen the gun ports when the guns were dragged back for reloading. These pendulums had also to be heaved aside with block and tackle before the gun could be run out again.

The pilot house was built log cabin-fashion of heavy iron members 9 by 12 inches, with the corners dove-tailed and bolted. It was set well forward on the deck with no communication with the turret except through a speaking tube. This voice pipe was found to be unreliable and the position of the pilot house prevented firing ahead. In all later monitors the pilot house was put on top of the turret. In the circumstances, the 16 men who toiled in the strange revolving box did not do badly.

According to Confederate (Southern) records, at one time during the fight the *Monitor* took up a position where the *Merrimac* could not bring a single gun to bear on her. The Confederates were surprised that their little opponent did not keep to this advantageous position.

The reason was that there were not the same facilities on the *Monitor* as there were on a big high vessel for observing clearly what the enemy was doing; and at times the revolving turret completely shut out the gunners' view of their target and they had to depend on messages brought from the pilot house to learn the exact position of the enemy. Thus, to a great extent the turret gunners fought in the dark and the vessel's superiority in manoeuvring ability did not compensate for these disadvantages.

The *Monitor* was struck 22 times, the pilot house twice, turret nine times, deck and sides three times each. The only vulnerable point was the pilot house. It was the shot that cracked one of the iron 'logs' of the pilot house which injured the *Monitor*'s captain. Two men in the turret were injured by concussion but no one was killed in the engagement.

Although neither vessel could be said to have won, morally the advantage lay with the *Monitor*, for it was her arrival at a critical moment which prevented the *Merrimac* from smashing every Federal ship in Hampton Roads, as this part of the mouth of the James River is known.

But the *Monitor* was fated to have a short existence. After taking part in several actions against shore batteries and carrying out patrol duty during the rest of the year 1862, she foundered in heavy weather on 31 December about 20 miles south-south-west of Cape Hatteras.

It was largely a repetition of her earlier experience in a gale. Water came in under the turret and through the hawse pipes and gained steadily until it washed against the grate bars of the furnaces. Steam pressure dropped and her escort vessel – the *Rhode Island* – began the difficult and dangerous work of taking off her crew by boats; but before rescue was completed she went down with four officers and 12 men who were still to be taken off. Like HMS *Captain*, she met her end soon after midnight.

It was reported that a serious leak was sprung in her by the pounding of the sea against the overhanging deck which was forced away from the top of the submerged hull. A contributing factor was probably her flat bottom and she, being too heavy to rise easily, had to absorb the full impact, which was more than such a vessel could take for long.

Much the same sort of effect was experienced by the flat-bottomed, shallow draft tank landing craft of the 1939–45 war. From the aft-mounted bridge of the LCTs the long flat deck could be seen to bend or bulge when the ship was severely struck by waves under the shallow flat bottom fore and aft. The heavy girders – or steel frames – about which the rectangular hulls were built were sometimes visibly warped after a heavy pounding.

Ericsson was not mistaken in predicting that the exploits of his *Monitor* would serve as a lesson to the governments of Europe. The United States had been slow to follow the trend towards building iron ships but now, as the only nation not only to have produced a revolutionary form of ship but actually to have tried it in real combat, she had signalled the irreversible end of wooden ships of war.

Captain Coles was not alone in writing to the press about the battle in Hampton Roads. He claimed that Ericsson's turret was based on his design but, since it is known that the Swedish engineer had prepared such a model before the Crimean War, it seems more likely that the two men had their brilliant idea independently.

The *Merrimac*'s depredations before the *Monitor* arrived lent support to a coastal defence opinion that Coles held. He advocated a fleet of turret ships of his design instead of fixed batteries to defend important installations.

"Mark the effect produced on the people of New York," Coles wrote, "when it was known that one solitary ironclad vessel, the *Merrimac*, had passed the fire of the Federal batteries without having received the slightest damage, had sunk and dispersed a wooden squadron and had gained for the time being entire control of the coast. A panic was the consequence. They felt at New York that their batteries were useless against a monster from whose sides the heaviest balls glanced off like hailstones and they were only restrained from the desperate and degrading alternative of blocking up their harbour by the telegram which informed them that the progress of the iron monster had been arrested by another iron ship, the *Monitor*.

"Let us pause for a moment and transfer these scenes to our own shores:

let us imagine at Portsmouth or London, for instance, the intelligence has been received of the approach of one of these iron monsters; let us suppose that the forts (at Spithead) upon which so much is to be spent and on which our safety is to be based, have been erected and that the Fleet (one of the conditions urged for the forts' erection) is absent. What protection would these forts at Spithead be against such vessels, which need never come within 1000 yards of these forts and at the same time be within good bombarding distance of the dockyard?"

But to Captain Coles, perhaps the most satisfactory aspect of the *Merrimac–Monitor* encounter was that the *Monitor*, with two heavy guns in its movable turret, had been able to take on a bigger ship armed with guns on the broadside principle.

This was the vindication of his theory which had already been tested on the range and expounded in lecture after lecture, letter after letter. After this the value of his invention for coastal defence was not doubted, indeed it had already been largely accepted; but the fatal acceptance of his principle in a sea-going steam and sailing ship was yet to come.

CHAPTER 5

THE FATAL DECISION

By April 1862, after further exchanges of letters with the Admiralty, Captain Coles threw down his public challenge in a letter to *The Times*. It was largely a repetition of his earlier letter to the Admiralty.

"I will repeat what I undertake to do should I only be allowed the opportunity. I propose to build two distinct classes of vessels; one to replace our wooden frigates and liners for sea-going purposes; and the other a totally different and smaller vessel or steamer raft for coast and local defence. I now wish to state further that I will undertake to prove that on my principle, a vessel shall be built nearly 100 feet shorter than the *Warrior*, and in all respects equal to her, with one exception, that I will undertake to disable and capture her within an hour. She shall draw four feet less water, require only half the crew and cost the country for building, at least £100,000 less. I am ready to stand or fall by these assertions."

But if the Admiralty were not yet ready to experiment with a sea-going turret ship, they were at least pressing ahead with another of Coles's ideas, the conversion of outmoded wooden battleships into mastless turret ships for coast defence. In this same month of April the Board authorized the cutting down of a recently completed three-deck ship, the *Royal Sovereign*. She originally mounted 131 guns in three tiers and was cut down to one deck carrying four Coles turrets.

Work began on her in April 1862, three weeks before the keel of the *Prince Albert* was laid. Although, therefore, two ships were being constructed to carry his inventions, Coles was not satisfied with this limited employment of his turrets. They had to sail the seven seas. He continued his campaign and chafed at the delay in completing the conversion of *Royal Sovereign*, which was not actually ready until the summer of 1864, some 18 months before the iron *Prince Albert* was to join the Fleet. So perhaps Coles's impatience is understandable.

It was nearly a year since the *Monitor* had fought the *Merrimac* and doubtless it was not Coles's advocacy alone that had influenced the Admiralty to experiment with the cut-down *Royal Sovereign*. The lesson of the battle was plain to anyone: but Whitehall was not to be hurried. Coles's principle was being applied in ships that were being built in private shipyards for foreign powers and their Lordships decided to wait and see; not only how *Royal Sovereign* behaved but how these private orders turned out as well.

In the event, the *Royal Sovereign* proved a success: her commander, Captain Sherard Osborn, an old friend of Coles, spoke highly of his novel vessel. She went on three weeks' trial in the English Channel between 28 August and 17 September 1864 and Osborn reported:

"The great width of deck is a serious defect but that is purely owing to this ship being a converted vessel. No vessel expressly constructed to carry turrets requires such a deck as we have, some 63 feet in width."

This great beam had been necessary because of the ponderous weight of three tiers of guns which the old *Royal Sovereign* was designed to carry on each side.

Osborn continued: "When rolling in a seaway, so wide a deck as ours, with a low bulwark, has an insecure appearance and, when riding at anchor in bad weather, the drift and wet blow along it in a very trying manner, severely punishing those exposed in charge of the watch. Fortunately, however, the crew of the *Royal Sovereign* – it having no masts or yards – need be little exposed to weather except for the lead and lookout."

It was to take an unparalleled disaster to convince the Admiralty that mastless ships could also be sent safely and efficiently wherever their duty might call them in any part of the world. But, as yet, masts and sails were still considered essential for long-distance cruising.

"The turrets and guns work admirably," reported Captain Osborn, "and we have now fired 177 rounds under all conditions. The rolling of the ship does not affect the evolutions of either turret or guns. The only defect I can observe exist is in the gun carriages being of wood instead of iron, and the necessity for a winch to run the guns in and out with, instead of the old-fashioned tackle: both these defects are in course of being remedied.

"The aperture cut through the upper deck to allow the turrets to revolve upon the lower deck instead of on the upper deck as in the case of the American monitors, requires to be secured or covered in upon a better principle than has yet been adopted. It involves the comfort and health of the crew owing to the admission of much wet and damp between the decks when fighting in a seaway."

Osborn's final judgement on the *Royal Sovereign* may have gone some way towards persuading the Admiralty in the end to give Coles freedom to build his own ship.

"I am of opinion," Osborn wrote, "that the *Royal Sovereign*, as she now stands, is the most formidable vessel of war I have ever been aboard of. She would easily destroy, if her guns were rifled, any of our present iron-clads, whether of the *Warrior, Hector*, or *Research* class. Her handiness, speed, weight of broadside and the small target she offers increase tenfold her powers of assault, and I believe I see my way to firing by night from a turret with as much accuracy as by day, so long as the enemy is visible.

"Vessels like the *Royal Sovereign* are admirably calculated for the defence of the coasts, harbours and roadsteads of Great Britain.

"With 12 such converted vessels the Fleet might be sent abroad to fight an enemy and we could feel secure at home, come what might – the more so as any naval officer would undertake to work and fight these vessels if manned by artillerymen, with only a dozen sailors to steer and take the lead."

The *Royal Sovereign* had four turrets, one containing two guns and the others one gun each. The success of the trials encouraged Coles to take a fairly strong line with the Admiralty, and to draw attention to the difference of opinion which existed between himself and the Chief Constructor of the Navy, E. J. Reed, who was naturally consulted by the Board of Admiralty whenever it was necessary to consider a proposal put forward by Coles.

The regularity of his proposals over the years and his public criticism of official shipbuilding policy, had led to a growing acrimony between him and Reed. But while accepting the value of turrets for limited use, as long as the Admiralty policy demanded sails as well as steam for ocean cruising, Reed was in favour of the broadside system of mounting guns on the ship's sides; but grouping them together amidships in a kind of armoured citadel which also acted as a shield to the engine room and magazine.

More than a year before the *Royal Sovereign* trials, at a time when Coles was impatient at delay in the ship's conversion, a request by him to have the assistance of an Admiralty draughtsman to prepare plans for a turret ship had been turned down by their Lordships. But they had said they were prepared "to give their best attention to any mature plan that might be submitted to them."

With the trials over and Osborn's resounding testimony behind him, Coles returned to the attack, not flinching from identifying Reed as the opponent of progress, as Coles saw it. He wrote to the Admiralty: "I am quite prepared to design a turret ship with proper assistance, and to do all I can further to develop and solve the problem of carrying the heaviest ordnance in a sea-going ship, for I might remark here that the turntable and turret principle is no longer a theory, but having been put

42

to practice, the question is now filtered down to a mere comparison as to which is the best of the two systems – the turntable with central armament, or guns on the extreme broadside.

"The decision on this point and the further adoption of my principle rests with their Lordships. I can only respectfully make my humble suggestions and use all my endeavours to overcome any difficulty that may present itself.

"The only difficulty that I see at present is that the Constructor of the Navy is opposed to the turret system, which he has publicly denounced, and is a strong advocate of his rival scheme."

The Admiralty now agreed to give Coles the assistance of Mr Scullard, Chief Draughtsman at Portsmouth dockyard, and invited Coles to submit "a design for a sea-going turret ship combining an armament of the heaviest guns with high speed and good sea-going qualities."

At the same time as Coles had been pressing his claims on the Admiralty there had been considerable support in the Press which, on the whole, tended to label E. J. Reed as a reactionary designer who was jealous of and resistant to the obvious quality of Coles, the gifted non-professional. This seems to have been an unfair assessment of Reed, who, there is no doubt, genuinely held his beliefs and was not a man to hazard the Navy's efficiency for the sake of a personal issue.

But being a human being – even if a rather severely self-confident one – he was no doubt irritated by the persistence and the untiring and outspoken denunciation of his shipbuilding principles by the half-pay captain-inventor.

These facts are clear from the vantage point of more than a century later, but at the time the two men existed in the public mind in uncompromising black and white – Reed black and Coles white.

Nor were Members of Parliament less restrained in their advocacy of Coles's ideas. Each naval occasion in the House of Commons (or Lords) brought forth its crop of speeches criticizing the government's naval plans.

Typical of them were the speeches of Mr Laird, friend of Coles, and a member of the shipbuilding firm which eventually built the *Captain.*

In the debate on the Naval Estimates for 1864 Mr Laird said: "Cupola ships are admirably adapted for going to sea and it would be a great injustice to Captain Coles, as well as a great loss to the country, if their powers in that respect were not put to the test. It is the duty of the Navy to test the invention and, if it answers, go on with it: if not, try something else."

Sir John Elphinstone, in the same debate, said:

"As to Captain Cowper Coles, he has provided a plan which produces easiness of motion, and speed, while carrying guns so high out of the water as to give a greater rate of fire than any other method with which we are acquainted. It is the duty of the government to have let Captain Coles lay down a complete plan of a cupola ship and to have finished a ship upon the plan so given so as to test the principle."

There were many other similar speeches and editorials in the newspapers. The government now decided to submit the whole question to a committee of naval experts under the chairmanship of Vice-Admiral Lord Lauderdale. This committee, which was appointed in 1865, considered the plan submitted by Coles in collaboration with Mr Scullard for a sea-going turret ship with one turret only. The Turret Ship Committee reported to the Admiralty in the following June.

They were against a turret ship having its armament in one turret on the grounds that it might be put out of action and leave the ship defenceless. But there had been such division of opinion on the question whether a turret ship could be made a satisfactory ocean cruising vessel that they recommended "a conclusive trial should be given to the system in a sea-going ship, to be armed with two turrets capable of carrying two 12-ton guns in each turret or, if necessary, one 22-ton gun in each."

The Admiralty accepted the committee's suggestion and instructed Vice-Admiral Sir Spencer Robinson, the Controller of the Navy, to let them know what he recommended for such a ship.

On 13 July the Controller, having discussed the matter with E. J. Reed, reported to their Lordships. He recommended, among other things, that a turret ship's main deck should be at least 16 feet above the waterline.

In the October following the Board of Admiralty instructed the Controller to prepare plans for a ship whose deck should be "not less than 14 feet above the waterline, and the turret gun ports should be 6 to 12 inches above the deck."

They also directed that the idea of complete all-round fire should be abandoned to the extent that direct forward firing should give way to a forecastle that would raise the ship's bows and so protect the deck from seas that would otherwise break clear on to it; and a poop – or stern structure – was to give the same protection and additional buoyancy at the stern.

The two turrets were to be placed amidships and as close together as possible. Thus the guns would be able to fire *nearly* straight ahead, just missing the forecastle, and *nearly* straight astern, just missing the poop – but by no means directly so.

To give complete protection directly fore and aft there were to be additional guns at the bow and stern; but these were not to be in turrets although they could be fitted with a shield to give some protection to the gunners.

In this way the Admiralty instructions defined the kind of ship that was to be designed. The result was HMS *Monarch*, designed by E. J. Reed. He never claimed to be enthusiastic about this ship and regarded it simply as something that met the requirements laid down by the Board.

Captain Coles was consulted before the design was prepared and he submitted plans for two turrets, to carry two 600-pounder guns each. There was considerable correspondence between Coles and the Controller before the ship's design was completed; but Coles's only part in the work was to supply details of his turrets. The actual responsibility for the ship was Reed's.

In September 1865, in a letter to Coles, the Admiralty had undertaken to let him see any design for a sea-going turret ship that might be produced by the Admiralty Constructor's department so that he might comment on it.

On 10 January 1866 the Controller submitted the officially produced design for the *Monarch* to the Board of Admiralty with the suggestion that "notwithstanding all that has passed, that a tracing of this design should be forwarded to Captain Coles for any observations he may wish to make upon it." There is no doubt, in view of their undertaking to Coles, that their Lordships would have done this. But Coles, not in the best of health and at the end of his patience with what he could only discern as the dilatoriness of the Admiralty, wrote a scathing letter to the Press, attacking Reed and throwing the blame for delay in building a sea-going turret ship on the Chief Constructor.

By ironic chance, this letter was published on the same day as the Controller submitted his *Monarch* design to the Board of Admiralty. After decrying the *Bellerophon* and the *Pallas*, two Reed-designed ships that had had to be expensively modified after their first trials, Coles wrote:

"I like opposition with fair play; it elucidates the truth. But has this opposition been fair to the country or have I met with fair play? Give me a hundredth part of the encouragement and assistance Mr Reed is given, and I think we could turn out a sea-going ship with as much despatch as *Pallas* or *Bellerophon* and ensure her being as great a success in her way as the *Royal Sovereign* has been in hers.

"Whilst speaking of designing ships, I care not who designs turret ships so long as the naval architect takes the matter up *con amore*, and is competent. The success of those vessels already built is due to the shipbuilder who designed them. I can only wish Mr Reed may be equally successful in the designs for the Admiralty turret ship, of which at present I can offer no opinion, not having seen the drawings." And Coles wrote a great deal more in similar vein.

The Board of Admiralty must have regarded this letter as the breaking point. They wrote to Coles reminding him that they had "more than once had occasion to disapprove of the course pursued by you in reference to your plans, and regret that instead of cordially co-operating with the Controller of the Navy in the endeavours to solve a most difficult problem, you have preferred to publish disingenuous statements and reflections on officers employed under the Board of Admiralty. Every allowance has been made for you as an inventor and as the advocate of your own plans; and my Lords have, therefore, abstained from noticing publications in which, whilst employed under the Board of Admiralty and receiving special pay for your services, you have, nevertheless, repeatedly attacked in the public Press the officers of the department with whom you have been requested to co-operate.

"My Lords had hoped that their forbearance would not have been misunderstood, but the tone and spirit of your letter of the 10th inst. have destroyed any such hope, and my Lords can no longer expect any useful co-operation or harmonious working between you and the officers of the Controller's department.

"My Lords regret that they can no longer sanction your employment in connection with the department which is engaged in the construction of a sea-going turret ship, since it is manifest that all friendly and confidential communications between you and the officers with whom you should have acted, are rendered impossible by the course you have deliberately pursued.

"My Lords are therefore compelled to cancel the order which had been given for allowing you the opportunity of inspecting and advising upon the plans for a sea-going turret ship, which have now been completed. The allowances made to you for your services in connection with building and fitting turret ships will therefore cease from this date."

Despair must have settled over the ailing inventor, whose pen was his worse disability, as he read this long and severely couched letter. He lost no time in apologizing and after further humble replies to further Admiralty letters, the Board relented and on 22 February 1866, accepted his "expression of regret at conduct which they have been obliged to take such serious notice of." They thereupon sent Coles the *Monarch* plans and invited him to comment on them. About six weeks later, on 17 April, Captain Coles gave the Admiralty his considered opinion.

"Allow me to observe," he wrote, "that in designing this ship one of the chief merits of the turret system, that of firing right ahead with her heaviest guns, appears to have been discarded, and the broadside plan substituted . . .

"I must therefore most respectfully but earnestly record my opinion that a sea-going turret ship should not be loaded with the bow and stern weight as proposed in the *Monarch*; that her turrets should not be deprived of the fore and aft fire, and that it is disadvantageous and unnecessary to add to her tonnage by giving her guns the unprecedented height of 17 feet out of water, tending to make her top-heavy and to labour heavily in a sea way . . .

"I think their Lordships will see that the *Monarch*, as now designed, cannot be said to represent my views of a sea-going turret ship, nor can she give my principle a satisfactory and conclusive trial."

He also made various suggestions for altering the armament, lowering the freeboard two feet, removing the forecastle, and forwarded a drawing of his proposals. E. J. Reed was to have bitter cause to recall this letter.

The Admiralty replied to Coles that the features he objected to were those resulting from the Board's instruction to the Controller and they were not prepared to abandon these decisions, which had been deliberately arrived at, and to substitute an entirely new design.

But in their next paragraph the Lords of the Admiralty, unwitting arbiters of the fates of Coles, Burgoyne and 500 others, made their unexpected but long-hoped-for decision. They agreed to the building of a ship to Coles's design.

How Coles's spirits must have soared as his eyes moved on from what seemed yet another refusal to pay attention to his ideas, to the words: "As, however, in your letter of the 3rd instant, you expressed your readiness to design a ship with two turrets, and you have now stated that you have several methods by which the desired objects may be attained, my Lords will give you the opportunity of reducing to practice your own views of what a sea-going turret ship should be, and they will authorize you to put yourself in communication with any of the firms named in the accompanying list, and to submit a design for a sea-going ship to carry not less than two turrets.

"Should my Lords be able to approve the design, and should they receive from the firm selected such a tender as they would feel themselves justified in accepting, they would then propose to Parliament that provision should be made in next year's Estimates for building such a vessel by contract."

The years of impatient but persistent pleading of his ideas had not, after all, been wasted. Coles lost no time. He wrote immediately to Lairds of Birkenhead, who were experienced in the building of turret ships, and they prepared a design.

It was for a ship with sides only eight feet above the water, compared with the *Monarch*'s 14 feet.

CHAPTER 6

THE SITTING DUCK

While the Admiralty were still considering this design, and some weeks before they finally approved the building of *Captain*, there occurred a highly popular public spectacle in the seemingly endless struggle between Coles and their Lordships in Whitehall.

It was nothing less than a practical test of the strength and vulnerability of one of Coles's turrets as fitted to the converted *Royal Sovereign*, which Captain Osborn had praised so much while commanding her. The Admiralty arranged that the *Bellerophon*, one of Reed's much criticised ships, armed on the broadside principle but with the guns grouped centrally behind armour, should fire on the *Royal Sovereign*'s aft turret and see what happened.

The turrets fitted to the *Royal Sovereign* were of Coles's early design, constructed to withstand the size and type of gun in use at sea a few years previously. But the gun on the *Bellerophon*, to be used against the turret, was of the latest design, a 12½-ton piece with rifled barrel: and it was to fire non-explosive shells weighing 250 lb, from a range of 150 yards. It seemed a rather unequal contest from the start, and Coles said so. But he had not been consulted about the test until the last moment and although his protests were no doubt noted, they were ignored.

To make matters even more adverse for the turret, its gun was removed and a wooden one substituted, the difference in weight in the turret being made up by solid shot stacked inside. Coles pointed out with justification, that taking out the gun left a vulnerable hole in the turret that was normally occupied by the gun barrel which served incidentally to deflect shots that might otherwise enter the turret by way of the gun port. This protest was also disregarded and the test duly took place off the Isle of Wight on Friday, 15 June 1866.

It was known as the Turret v Broadside test; somewhat inaccurately, because not only was it an unequal contest for the reasons given, but it was simply a test of the strength of the turret: the turret was not to, and could not, fire back. It was suggested in the Press afterwards that it might be thought reasonable to let the *Royal Sovereign* send one or two shots at

Bellerophon to test Reed's system of putting armour plate round his centrally grouped guns. But, understandably, their Lordships ignored this irreverent suggestion.

The Turret v Broadside test was a great public occasion, and a description of it is best left to the Press reporter who was there:

"The experiment has created universal interest," he wrote. "The public have sympathized with Captain Coles and on many occasions sympathy has found vent in unmistakable terms . . ."

The *Royal Sovereign* was anchored off the eastern end of the island beyond the Nab Light. Our correspondent was aboard the *Bellerophon* when she took up her position 150 yards from the *Royal Sovereign* and broadside on. It was a busy and summery scene:

"About and around were innumerable yachts of every description, from the tiny boat – cutter-rigged, to the handsome clipper schooner with her white spreading canvas. Numerous steamers arrived about two, crowded with passengers anxious to witness the experiment . . . The *Osborne* yacht hove in sight about three o'clock with the Lords Commissioners of the Admiralty on board . . . By four o'clock their Lordships had assembled on the bridge of the *Bellerophon* and her bulwarks and rigging were crowded with visitors and seamen, all eyes being turned anxiously towards the little turret of the *Royal Sovereign.*"

To the enquiry from *Bellerophon,* "Are you ready?" came the prompt reply, "The sooner the better." The *Royal Sovereign* was manned during the test, but those on board took shelter in the forward turrets. Even so, there were pessimistic prophecies of what might happen to them when the firing commenced. The whole proceeding had about it that same element of excitement which is created by a dangerous circus act.

"The deck of the turret ship was quickly cleared and the vessel lay steadily waiting for what all believed would be a terrible pounding. Captain Coles did not hesitate to express his opinion that the great shot would do much damage. He expressed confidence in the rotary gear but still protested against the removal of the gun. . . . All eyes were turned towards the *Royal Sovereign* when suddenly a sharp ringing report was heard, and then a whizz and a whirl informed us that the first shot had left the muzzle of the monster cannon."

This first shot carried away a piece of target that had been set up on top of the turret to aid the gunners. Coles was standing with the Duke of Somerset, First Lord of the Admiralty and, according to a reporter of the scene, Coles made "an amusing observation" after the first shot. Coles had had years of wordy warfare with the Admiralty from which to draw for some suitable remark about a shot that only just managed to clip the edge of a large target at such close range. It is not difficult to imagine his offering to do better with his somewhat elderly turret against the *Bellerophon*, with the First Lord's permission. Whatever he said, the Duke was seen to answer good-humouredly.

"Another bang and a sudden blow and crack told us that this shot, the first aimed at the turret itself, had done its work of destruction. The shot struck the turret where Coles had prophesied, at the weakest point, the side of the gun port . . . and the Lords of the Admiralty, the officials and visitors went on board to discover the amount of damage done."

It was found that the solid shot had pierced the 5½-inch iron plate round the gun port, and had glanced in, smashing the dummy gun. Several plates were displaced by the shot and several bolts started. It is probable that if the turret had had its real gun in position the shot would not have entered. But despite the damage it was found that the turret was still in working order and could be turned.

Now that it was seen not to be unduly dangerous to remain on board, the distinguished observers crowded into the forward turrets of the *Royal Sovereign* while a third and fourth shot were fired at the aft turret. The official party again examined the turret. It was still more battered and a chunk of iron had been gouged out of it by a glancing shot. Coles operated the turret turning mechanism and the great iron cylinder rumbled round with no sign that it had just been playing the role of a sitting duck for the Navy's latest and most destructive gun.

One of the shots had been deliberately aimed at the deck just in front of the turret in the hope of damaging the turning mechanism – since this was one of the main objects of the test, to see whether the turret could be put out of action – but it merely glanced off, damaging but not disabling. Coles spun the turret at full speed and could not forbear to cry: "The works are uninjured."

Although it was obvious from the test that the turret might even be virtually demolished in time, it was equally clear that no amount of damage to the gunners' shield would affect the manoeuvrability of their guns, and so long as they remained intact and sufficient men survived to serve them – the inevitable conditions of combat – they could be worked. Thus the imponderable question about Coles's turrets – was their turning mechanism vulnerable in action? – seemed to a great extent answered; and this criticism, at least, could be silenced.

Although the Admiralty had already agreed in principle to the building of a sea-going turret ship to Coles's design, there can be no doubt that the outcome of this spectacular test must have been reassuring to them, since the only reason for building the proposed ship was to carry the turret – in its latest form – which had been so triumphantly demonstrated. Coles, no doubt, was also pleased as he joined the official party, still

50

peering and discussing the damage done during the test.

The unknown reporter here added a touch of colour to his account: "An amusing incident occurred at this time concerning a steam boat with excursionists on board who were not only desirous, but overanxious to see the effect of the last shot. The Duke of Somerset and several of the Board of Admiralty were minutely inspecting the damage when His Grace and party were requested, in the most common language, to get on one side and allow the excursionists to have 'their see, too.' The request was shortly afterwards complied with and the party on board the steamer expressed their gratitude by giving three hearty cheers."

It was a typically English incident and one that graphically expresses the air of unofficial carnival that the holiday-making public imposed upon the otherwise serious official proceedings.

A week later the same writer, referring to the success of the test, recalled that "Captain Coles was not satisfied with the conditions laid down for the trial. He protested, not on personal grounds, but upon grounds of equity and fair play. He cared not for himself, but having confidence in his principle, if fairly tested, he demurred to the conditions of a trial that might, by reason of its unfairness, tend to prejudice the turret system in the minds of an observing people.

"We are all aware that Captain Coles has been anxious that his system should be thoroughly tested in order, if possible, to settle a question that has given him no end of trouble, anxiety and suffering, both physical and mental. When it was rumoured that the system was to be finally submitted to a trial, the inventor, having the greatest confidence in his work, gladly welcomed it and waited for instructions. But the Admiralty have ever shown themselves to be anxious that Captain Coles should steer clear of them: they do not even like necessary contiguity, which fact has been proved in the past.

"The inventor of the cupola and turret system has manfully fought his battle, backed by public opinion on shore and afloat; and inch by inch my Lords have reluctantly been compelled to yield. In proof of this, your readers will remember that it was only by force of public opinion that Captain Coles received permission to build a turret ship after his own designs: and unless a reliance on the inventor's genius is somewhat visionary and his skill much exaggerated, the *Captain* will, when finished by Messrs Lairds, be the most effective ship of the British Navy."

This was a typical sample of Press support for Coles, born of the nation's instinctive sympathy for the lone man against bureaucracy. It was strengthened by the fact that Reed's ships did not always come up to expectations, and sometimes modifications had to be made to them. But it was, of course, a time of advance in ship design and no man could dogmatically forecast a ship's performance, when she differed from previous vessels significantly, until she was afloat and under way.

However, the fact that it was a time, to some extent, of trial and error, made it seem to the public unreasonable that the official constructors could build ship after ship that might not turn out to be wholly satisfactory, while Coles, with his seemingly dramatic and exciting idea, could not get one vessel built to demonstrate it on an adequate scale.

CHAPTER 7

DESIGN FOR DISASTER

The *Captain*, designed to be built with lower sides than was usual, saved a great deal of top weight; and so she could be made less wide than Reed's *Monarch*. This is because the heavier a ship is the greater must be the volume of its hull and the consequent balancing weight of water displaced to support the hull's weight. The *Captain*'s slimmer form also meant that it could be powered by smaller engines – 900 horsepower, compared with the *Monarch*'s 1100 horsepower.

In his preliminary report on the plans, which were submitted to him by the Board of Admiralty, E. J. Reed commented: "I am satisfied that the ship is well designed and proportioned, and that her dimensions are not unduly large for the weights to be carried and the speed to be attained. I do not think she differs very materially in these respects from what would have been proposed in this department had their Lordships seen fit to sanction in our design an upper deck eight feet above the water."

It was only a preliminary look at the design but Reed could not resist pointing out that he had recommended something of this kind to Coles nearly two years earlier, when they had been trying to reach a compromise between Coles's advocacy of all-round fire and flush decks and Reed's caution in committing himself to such a design for ocean cruising.

Remembering Coles's letter about the plans for the *Monarch*, he drew attention to the fact that although Coles had been very critical of the officially designed ship because it had a forecastle which interfered with the forward fire of the turrets, the newly proposed ship had precisely the same feature – a forecastle and a poop and consequent limited fire fore and aft.

In this aspect of the design Coles had had to give way to the superior knowledge and experience of Lairds, who had built turret ships for foreign navies. They had found that a low freeboard vessel could not use her guns in a seaway when awash and that only a built-up bow and stern could keep the deck moderately dry. Thus Coles had to forgo this important element of all-round fire: and Reed's irritation may be understood.

Reed thought that the weights allowed for in the design seemed on the low side, but would probably be all right. However, he warned against the use of too much iron in the structure. On the whole, his criticism was restrained and he does not appear to have tried to belittle the plan.

But in forwarding Reed's report to the Board of Admiralty, his superior, the Controller of the Navy, remarked: "I am doubtful whether the proposed height of the upper deck out of the water, *viz.* eight feet, combined with the length and draught of water of this design, will be satisfactory for a sea-going cruising ship."

On 23 July 1866 Coles received the long-awaited official approval: "My Lords approve of a ship being built on the entire responsibility of yourself and Messrs Lairds, but the works will be carried on under the usual Admiralty inspection as to workmanship and materials."

Coles replied the next day, almost exuberantly: "I am not only ready to accept any joint responsibility which may fairly belong to me, but should be ready to take the sole responsibility of strongly recommending their Lordships to build this ship as designed; but as regards contracts, prices, or any matters other than the design itself, the responsibility, of course, will rest with Messrs Lairds."

Meanwhile E. J. Reed was examining the ship plans more carefully, as he had been instructed to do by the Board of Admiralty. He made his more considered report on 2 August 1866. He pointed out that as Admiralty supervision of the building was to be limited to the quality of materials used and workmanship, it was possible that structural arrangements in the hull might not be up to the standard he would otherwise have insisted upon. This was merely a general warning – a safeguard for himself, it may be thought. But there then followed the first instance of official wisdom before the event.

Reed wrote: "The hull appears to me to be somewhat heavily designed in places, and the weight allowed for barely sufficient, and if any suggestions of mine led to increased weight occasion might thus be afforded for a transfer to this department of a responsibility which does not belong to it, *in the event of the ship proving too deeply immersed.*" The italics are the author's.

Reed also pointed out that Laird's specifications for the weights of auxiliary engines required to turn the turrets and work the capstans had not been included in the design. His report concluded with a paragraph which was truly prophetic and, in retrospect, it is scarcely conceivable that not only this warning, but other more specific evidence of danger which came later, should have been so completely ignored.

"It also appears to me desirable," wrote Reed, "that their (Lairds') attention should be called to the probable position of the centre of gravity, as regards height. In my preliminary report I expressed no doubt as to the stability of the ship, but on investigating the matter I find that the centre of gravity of ships armed and plated in the proposed manner is situated higher than would appear probable at first sight, and I would advise that Messrs Lairds be requested thoroughly to satisfy themselves on this point, *especially as it is proposed to spread a large surface of canvas upon the Captain.*"

Again, the italics are the author's, but it is well to realize that these observations of Reed, who was often slated in Press and Parliament, were made when the *Captain* was no more than lines and calculations on sheets of paper.

The Admiralty passed on these warnings about weight and centre of gravity to Lairds, who replied that they had carefully considered these points "and have no reason to fear that the vessel will be deficient in the stability necessary. We may observe that in the event of the vessel being light with all coals burnt out, it is provided that the space under the double bottom may be filled with water as ballast."

After further correspondence with Lairds and interviews with Coles, the Admiralty tried to get the inventor to agree to accept, with the builders, the entire responsibility for the new ship, Coles to have the same supervisory powers as the Controller of the Navy had for supervising the building in private yards of ships designed by his department.

Captain Coles raised certain objections which delayed matters for some weeks and finally, on 19 November 1866, he wrote to the Admiralty: "In consequence of recent illness I am obliged, under medical advice, to decline any responsibility or engagement which would involve my residence or attendance at Birkenhead in the winter or spring, and under these circumstances it would be useless further to discuss any arrangement of responsibility between Messrs Lairds and myself in reference to the *Captain* which would involve the necessity of such residence or attendance."

He also said that he could not undertake any responsibility beyond that of the design of the ship, which was his contribution to the experiment. He referred to Lairds' experience and quality as shipbuilders, implying that he was content to leave the execution of his design in their hands; but he offered to give any advice that might be needed upon the turret system itself.

There is no reason to suppose that Captain Coles was trying to evade responsibility in the matter. The fact is that he suffered from a chronic chest condition and Birkenhead in the winter was really no place for him. He had suggested that the ship be built in a Royal Naval Dockyard – which would probably have meant somewhere on the south coast – but the Admiralty preferred the matter to be in private hands.

The whole proceeding was unusual, to say the least. The Admiralty had decided that an experimental sea-going turret ship should be built, and they were prepared to pay for it; but they wanted to shift the entire responsibility for its success or failure to Captain Coles and Lairds, as the co-designers. It is difficult to see how their Lordships expected to divest themselves of their proper duty, but that was the situation when Coles made his own position clear.

The Board discussed this latest problem with Sir Spencer Robinson, Controller of the Navy, and on 23 November 1866 he suggested a solution:

"Their Lordships' directions to me as Controller of the Navy relieved me from all responsibility concerning this ship, except as to the workmanship and materials, which it was my duty to overlook as before with a view to secure their being in all respects fit for Her Majesty's Service.

"This responsibility did not extend to the design or to the specification, neither of which, as their Lordships are aware, met with my entire approval.

"The form of contract is now printing which gives Captain Coles all the necessary powers, and indeed all the powers possessed by the Controller of the Navy for ensuring the ship being built according to his design, and as Captain Coles declines to exercise these powers, I see no other way of proceeding than by inserting in every clause of the contract where Captain Coles has been named, the words 'Controller of the Navy . . .' I am fully aware how difficult and onerous such a position would prove. However careful I may be, and however painfully anxious to cause the ship to be built according to Captain Coles's wishes, the experience of five years has taught me how small a chance I have of succeeding, or of avoiding most unpleasant communications."

This bitter comment gives an insight of the extent to which Captain Coles had been a goad and source of unremitting trouble to the Controller's department. The even tenor of their way came to an end the day Coles sketched his first neat plan for taking the guns off his Crimea raft and putting them in ships to go to sea.

The department no doubt groaned every time the post brought one of his firmly written letters in black ink. They soon knew his sloping, slightly pointed handwriting at a glance. An annoyance he certainly was, and right he certainly was in the basic conception of his turret whose principle was, in the end, adopted universally. He was wrong only in his belief, based on an incomplete understanding of ship design, that the ship which was finally built was safe to put to sea: and in that error, which would cost him his life, he was not alone.

CHAPTER 8

BIRTH OF A SHIP

The contract for the building of the *Captain* was signed on 4 March 1867. Coles was no longer responsible for supervising the building; but Lairds of Birkenhead were still made "strictly responsible for the successful completion" of the ship. Coles was to advise on the installation of his gun mountings.

A Mr Hobbs, of the Constructor's Department, was sent to Birkenhead to superintend construction and give advice – if he was asked for it. But his chief duty was "to ascertain that the materials and workmanship are of the very best description and quality, and in strict accordance with the contract and with the usages of Her Majesty's Service."

But Hobbs was not to interfere in any way with the actual design of the vessel. Coles had given a written assurance that if it was built according to the plans submitted then it would "represent my views of what a sea-going turret ship ought to be, and that, if so carried out, I shall be satisfied that my principle has had a fair trial as far as this class of vessel is concerned."

Work proceeded without any serious hitches. But on 2 May 1867 the Controller made it quite clear that his department was not going to be involved in responsibility for the success or otherwise of the design.

Lairds had asked him to approve an increase in the size of iron beams used in the hull. Sir Spencer Robinson covered himself in his approval by saying: "My approval of such increase, or any additions to the weight of the hull which may hereafter be submitted to me for approval, must not in any way be construed into an approval of a departure from the aggregate weight of hull of that ship, for which weight, and for the load draught of water, you are of course responsible."

The first official murmur of alarm about the possible weight of the ship came on 4 September 1867, when Nathaniel Barnaby, one of Reed's assistants (and his eventual successor), visited Birkenhead.

He reported to Reed: "I found the work everywhere well and honestly done, but if I were responsible for the weight of the ship I should be greatly alarmed at the appearance everywhere of extravagance in the use of materials. There is no evidence anywhere of economy in either labour or materials." However, Barnaby said nothing to Lairds about this, and in fact, he may not have considered himself in a position to do so.

Towards the end of 1868 the third of the principal characters in the story of the *Captain* came upon the scene of her building. At the special request of Captain Coles, Captain Hugh Talbot Burgoyne, V.C., was appointed to the command of the new ship and joined her at Birkenhead to be present during the final stages of her construction.

Captain Hugh Burgoyne was born in 1833, the only son of Sir John Fox Burgoyne. Sir John was the eldest of four illegitimate children of Lieutenant-General the Rt Hon. John Burgoyne, uncle of the 12th Earl of Derby. When the General died in 1792 the four children were cared for by the Earl, and John Fox Burgoyne was sent to Eton. Although his illegitimate birth held him back from high honours in the early part of his life, he eventually became a Baronet, a Field Marshal and one of the most respected military figures of Victorian England.

All Sir John's hopes were centred on Captain Hugh, his only son. Hugh Burgoyne entered the Navy in 1847 as a midshipman and was promoted Lieutenant on 11 January 1854. The following March he was appointed to HMS *Boscawen*, a sailing man-of-war, and served in the Baltic. Six months later he returned to England, was posted to the *Swallow* and sailed for the Mediterranean and Black Sea, where the Crimean war had just broken out. Like Coles, he was attached to the Fleet before Sebastopol.

Burgoyne was 21 and chafing at the comparative inactivity of the ships. After Genitchi had been shelled, Burgoyne volunteered to land with two others and set fire to some Russian stores. A daring exploit, it was successfully carried out, although the three men had to run for their lives afterwards to reach their boat before a troop of Cossacks could cut them off from the beach.

For this action Burgoyne became one of the first men to be decorated with the Victoria Cross when it was instituted the following year. His lack of seniority prevented his being promoted at once, but he was appointed to command the *Wrangler*, a despatch gunboat, in which he served for the rest of the war. He was made Commander in May 1856, still only 23. After service in the Pacific he was promoted Captain in May 1861. In 1863 he accompanied Captain Sherard Osborn to China as second-in-command of the Anglo-Chinese flotilla, and the two men became close friends.

On Burgoyne's return to England he was appointed in September 1865 to the command of the *Wivern*, a small turret ship in which he served for the next two years. The *Wivern*, although a turret ship of low freeboard, was nothing to do with Captain Coles – except for the turrets. She was one of a pair of ships (the other was *Scorpion*) that had been the subject of friction between Britain and the North American States two years earlier.

The *Wivern* and the *Scorpion* were ordered from Lairds in March 1862 by Captain James D. Bullock, naval agent for the Confederate (Southern) States and they were intended to try and break the Northern States' blockade on the Southern ports. Bullock ordered the ships in his own name to conceal their real destination. When they were half built Lord John Russell, the Foreign Secretary, informed Bullock that he was aware of the true situation and that the ships would not be allowed to put to sea unless as the property of a nation not at war.

Bullock arranged with some French bankers to purchase the vessels on behalf of the Egyptian government and they were accordingly named *El Toussan* and *El Mounassir*. The real intention, however, was to transfer them at sea to Confederate agents.

When the Foreign Secretary learnt of this ruse the British government seized the ships and eventually purchased them for the British Navy, renaming them *Scorpion* and *Wivern*. The two ships were iron built, well armoured, fully rigged and fitted with rams on the bows. They became popularly known, for this reason, as the Birkenhead rams. They were not designed as world-wide cruisers, but *Wivern* gave Burgoyne useful experience of turret ships.

Burgoyne next served for a year in command of the frigate *Constance* on the North American station and, towards the end of 1868, when the *Constance* was paid off, he joined the *Captain* at Birkenhead.

The *Captain* was floated out of the dry dock on 27 March 1869. Mrs John Laird, jun. performed the naming ceremony, dashing the traditional bottle of wine against the ship's bows and wishing her luck. The First Lord of the Admiralty, now H. C. E. Childers, was among the large crowd of notables and sightseers who watched the ship float slowly out as the Lairds works band played suitable music. The distinguished visitors were taken on board the ship, which had steam raised, and they saw the turrets turned both by steam and by hand. They also watched the engines working. It was a day for compliments and polite curiosity.

Coles himself had been unable to attend the ceremony: but F. K. Barnes, the Assistant Constructor, was there, and it was only a few people, like him, who may have exchanged serious glances as they noticed that the ship was obviously floating deeper in the water than had been planned.

Work of fitting out went on during the following year; and the feeling between Coles and Reed at this time is occasionally seen in correspondence about Coles's expenses. Although he was not generally supervising the construction, as the Admiralty had at first wanted, he made frequent visits to Woolwich and London in connection with the making of the gun carriages and mountings. For this he was allowed to claim expenses. But when, in October 1869, he submitted the cost of his hotel bill as a travelling expense, the Admiralty objected.

E. J. Reed was asked by the Board for his opinion. It would probably be unjust to Reed to suppose that he allowed his vexation over Coles to lead him into making an adverse report. But there is a human factor in all relationships and it may be that if he and Coles had been on the best of terms he might not have replied to their Lordships in quite the way he did.

On the question of Coles's expenses Reed wrote: "I cannot say that this is satisfactory to my mind. It appears to me that an officer engaged by the Admiralty, as Captain Coles is engaged, and paid as he is paid, should be required to live not in the Isle of Wight, but near to his work. But the question appears to be one which should be carefully decided in view of the agreement cited by Captain Coles. No Admiralty officer is allowed to charge continuous subsistence allowance but, on the other hand, Captain Coles' employment is but temporary and he may fairly perhaps maintain the view he has taken."

Coles had, in fact, been authorized by the Admiralty in 1862, during the early days of his co-operation in the installation of turrets in various ships, to charge subsistence allowance while away from home on duty. It was this agreement to which he referred when supporting his claim to charge hotel bills indefinitely.

He wrote to the Admiralty: "I beg to explain that during the last quarter I have found it necessary with respect to the gun carriages and other matters connected with the *Captain* to be away from my residence in the Isle of Wight; and I remained in the vicinity of London that I might save time and expense of the numerous journeys I should have been obliged to make to and from the Isle of Wight, and enable me more readily to communicate in person with the Admiralty, Woolwich Gun Factory, The Royal Carriage Department and Laird Bros of Birkenhead. Therefore, while so employed away from my home in the Isle of Wight, under my agreement with the Lords Commissioners of the Admiralty dated 19 November 1862, I am entitled to the subsistence money charged in my account for the last quarter, in which you will observe that the three days whilst living on board the *Monarch* I have not charged."

Coles was an expert at this old game of justifying expenses. He had been through a similar argument with the Admiralty during the previous spring when he had charged for being away from home for 50 days. The meticulous noting of three days during which he lived on board a naval vessel was the kind of touch that W. S. Gilbert could have had in mind when he wrote in *The Mikado*: "Merely corroborative detail, intended to give artistic verisimilitude to an otherwise bald and unconvincing narrative."

Coles probably enjoyed these little battles with the Admiralty. He was not a wealthy man and had ten children at the time of his death, so he could not afford to be out of pocket. But he was a man who thrived on detail. He would have enjoyed pointing out the extreme accuracy of his expenses, just as he enjoyed to represent every bolt head and detail of construction in the fine models he made of his various inventions. He was also a gifted amateur artist, particularly of sea scenes.

Coles may have thought the Admiralty were being somewhat niggardly, since he was working very hard, whether he felt well or not. The ship that was being created was a powerful driving force; and even when confined to bed Coles worked on the details of mounting and installing the *Captain*'s 25-ton guns, spreading his papers over a plain deal table – made by himself – which stood by his bed.

Coles's expenses caused a considerable stir in the Admiralty. The Controller wrote about them to the First Lord:

"It is perfectly clear that the present arrangement with Captain Coles ought to come to an end as being highly disadvantageous for the public service. The agreement made with Captain Coles stipulates, *inter alia,* that for a defined period, *viz.* for 14 years from 1862 Captain Coles will, when required by the Admiralty, give them his services on being paid at the rate of £3.3s per day, and the travelling expenses referred to can only be claimed when Captain Coles is employed by their Lordships on their Lordships' business. While he is by their direction employed in superintending the construction of the *Captain* he is entitled to these payments and allowances. But when that work is completed he stands in the same position as any other officer, and if not employed he must fall back on half-pay.

"Within my knowledge there is no work connected with the Constructor's Department of the Admiralty on which Captain Coles could be permanently employed with advantage to the public service.

"Whenever it may be thought advisable to ask Captain Coles for an opinion, or for a suggestion about the details of his invention, for which every time it is used by the Admiralty he receives a royalty of £100, he must, according to the terms of the agreement, receive the pay and allowances already referred to – but he must be given to understand that these payments and allowances are not permanent and are awarded as per agreement for the time, and the time only, that he is employed on Admiralty business.

"The completion of the *Captain*, now close at hand, affords an excellent opportunity for giving Captain Coles notice of the Admiralty's intentions. The trials of the *Captain* which will soon take place will show the exact value of Captain Coles's services to the Admiralty. That ship has been designed and constructed on his entire responsibility and until her success has been satisfactorily established, first as to the qualities of the ship and her fulfilment of the recorded intentions of the designers, and secondly as to the efficient use she can make of her armament in the turrets, it would be premature to enter into any engagement whatever with Captain Coles, other than those to which the Admiralty have already bound themselves."

But no doubt the First Lord, being an enthusiastic supporter of Coles – and at loggerheads with E. J. Reed – paid less attention to the Controller's opinions on Coles's expenses and his future employment than the Controller would have wished.

It was December 1869. Within a year the quibble over what Coles was or was not entitled to charge as expenses would be resolved by his death.

*   *   *

Three days after the *Captain* was floated out of the building dock Mr Barnes reported to the Admiralty. He calculated that when she was complete and ready for sea, taking into account the amount she was already overweight, she would exceed her designed weight by 427 tons and would therefore float at least 13 inches deeper in the water than planned.

When E. J. Reed forwarded Barnes's report to the Board he pointed out that Barnes's calculations were based on Coles's original estimate of a crew of 400 men, whereas it was the Admiralty's view that a complement of 500 should be carried. Reed estimated that the additional men would increase the weight carried by about 50 tons, sinking the ship a further 1½ inches and reducing the height of the main deck above water to 6 feet 9½ inches. Their Lordships noted the report but did not refer it to either Lairds or Coles.

One man who was vaguely uneasy about the new ship, without really knowing why, was the man who was to have most reason to recall his misgivings – James May, the Gunner, one of the few who were to survive the coming disaster.

May was appointed to the *Captain* at Birkenhead in November 1868, nearly two years before her loss, one of the specially selected key men who, under Captain Burgoyne, were sent to the ship to form her first crew.

The ship was rigged at Birkenhead by a naval party from Portsmouth, the ropes being supplied by the government and the spars by the contractors. May recalled: "I was very much struck by the size and weight of her masts and yards. In fact, all her spars appeared to me to be too heavy, and I think there were many others who shared this opinion with me. I have often felt astonished when looking down from Bidston Hill, Birkenhead, as the ship lay in the great Float Dock, to see her masts towering many yards above everything else in the vicinity of the docks."

However, these were criticisms remembered *after* the ship had gone down. Until that day May had considered, with others, that he served in the finest vessel afloat.

On 24 February 1870 Lairds wrote to the Admiralty a letter which was to figure prominently in the inquiry into the disaster. It appears to betray a certain uneasiness on the part of the builders. Yet, strangely, it did not arouse the kind of prompt action by Reed that might, in retrospect, have been expected of him in view of his definite opinions about the stability of low-sided iron ships carrying a full rig of sails.

Lairds wrote: "Now that the *Captain* is completed, and before she proceeds to sea, a careful experiment should be made by inclining with weights in the steam basin to ascertain the position in a vertical direction of the centre of gravity with a greater certainty than is possible from calculation."

They pointed out that in the past similar experiments had been carried out with ironclad naval vessels, which had at first presented different seagoing characteristics from the traditional wooden ships.

Lairds went on: "As these ships differed from ships *not* armour-clad, so the *Captain* may be said to differ in many respects from *other* iron-clad ships, and hence our reason for requesting that their Lordships will allow similar experiments to be made with the *Captain*."

But Reed seemed to find no urgency in the matter, and despite his opposition to ships of the *Captain* design, there can be little doubt that he anticipated no immediate danger. He was not the kind of man who would have knowingly hazarded the lives of hundreds of men in the expectation of proving himself right and Coles wrong. In fact, the interest in the proposed experiment was more academic than anxious; imminent disaster was not in anyone's mind.

Reed advised the Board of Admiralty that the inclining experiment would be carried out when there was a suitable opportunity and the weather was more settled. "It is not considered desirable to attempt to carry out the experiment before the forthcoming steam trials are completed or while the weather is so unsettled," the Admiralty told Lairds.

After the trials, Mr Barnes reported on 5 March 1870 "the ship will certainly be at least 22 inches more immersed than was intended by her designers. This large departure from what was intended by the contract of the ship, raises the question whether the ship should be accepted in that condition by their Lordships."

The Admiralty did not, in fact, pay immediately and correspondence dragged on between Lairds and Whitehall and Coles. Reed, in advising the Admiralty to delay payment until the ship had proved herself at sea, said: "I consider this the more important because it is not impossible that Captain Coles may disclaim the vessel, and represent that she does not fulfil his intentions and expectations, notwithstanding the fact that he has systematically certified his satisfaction with the ship during the various stages of her progress up to the time of the last payment upon her being made."

On the question of the ship's excessive weight, Reed could not resist pointing out that "although it was no part of the duty of this department to advise or assist Messrs Laird on this question (as our responsibility was very strictly and carefully limited by their Lordships to the supervision of the quality of the materials and the workmanship), yet my officers were uniformly instructed to mention to Messrs Laird, as occasion might offer, what they more than once mentioned to me, and what I also saw myself upon my visits to the ship and mentioned to the firm, *viz* that throughout the building of the ship iron was put into her in larger quantities than would have been deemed requisite in the building of such a ship in Her Majesty's Dockyards, or under my directions. The responsibility there-fore of necessity rests entirely upon the contractors and Captain Coles."

The question then arose, had Lairds properly fulfilled their contract by building a ship that differed so much in its height of freeboard from the original plan?

They had been paid, as was usual, by instalments as the work progressed. The total contract price was £335,000 and by the time the *Captain* was floated out of the building dock there was £7650 still to be paid.

The Admiralty decided to withhold this last payment until the ship had proved herself, or otherwise. When, by 2 September 1870, it appeared that, despite the many misgivings, the *Captain* had demonstrated herself to be seaworthy, and an efficient fighting machine as well, the Admiralty finally authorized the settlement of the outstanding amount.

Captain Cowper Phipps Coles, C.B., R.N., inventor of the British turntable turret system of mounting guns in warships.

Sir Edward James Reed, Chief Constructor of the Navy, 1863–1870.
(*By kind permission of the Royal Institution of Naval Architects.*)

Captain Hugh Talbot Burgoyne, V.C., seated foreground with dog. The officer standing centre behind him is the Gunner, Mr James May. *(Courtesy of National Maritime Museum, Greenwich. Neg. No. A2544)*

HMS *Captain* in a Royal Dockyard during completion.
(Courtesy of Imperial War Museum, London. Neg. No. Q40607)

Mainmast

Mizzenmast

Yard

Maintopsail

Flying, or
Hurricane deck

Poop

Aft turret

Main deck

Fore turret

Hull model of HMS *Captain*, formerly in the Royal United Service Institution, London and now in the National Maritime Museum.
(Photo by Frank Pocklington)

Contemporary artist's impression of HMS *Captain* under the sail she was carrying on the night she foundered; and showing the main ship terms used in her story.
(Courtesy of National Maritime Museum, Greenwich. Neg. No. N338)

ast

oretopsail

il & rigging control ropes
neets, halliards, braces

Foretopmast staysail

ecastle

One of the turrets of HMS *Captain* and the underside of the hurricane deck.
(Courtesy of National Maritime Museum, Greenwich. Neg. No. 7110)

Fore part of model of HMS *Captain*, formerly in the Royal United Service Institution, showing fore turret and, above it, the boat in which the survivors escaped. *Note:* The funnel of the ship, which could be lowered when sails were in use, is in the 'down' position. *(Photo by Frank Pocklington)*

CHAPTER 9

A SHIP TO SWEEP
THE SEAS

The *Captain* had her steam trials in March 1870 and Coles was on board for the customary run over a measured mile. Her average speed was 14.239 knots. It was a very satisfactory result, better than had been expected of her and much better than some of her critics had been forecasting. In fact, her mean speed was nearly equal to the *Monarch*, which had averaged 14.937 knots, but was a bigger ship – 5102 tons compared to the *Captain*'s 4272 tons – and with more powerful engines.

HMS *Captain* was commissioned at Portsmouth on Saturday, 30 April. By one of those curious fancies of Fate the ensign was hoisted wrong way up the first time it was flown – normally a signal of distress. The omen of ill luck was quickly noticed and the flag righted; but seldom has a sign of bad luck been so tragically fulfilled – there would be no time for distress signals.

The *Captain* sailed a few days later with the *Monarch* and the *Volage* to rendezvous with the Channel Fleet – under command of Vice-Admiral Sir Thomas Symonds – at a point 30 miles westward of Cape Finisterre, where they were due on Saturday, 21 May.

Coles was on board the *Captain* at the invitation of the Admiralty, and before he sailed he had a long talk with his old friend Captain Sherard Osborn, after whom he had named one of his sons.*

At this time Coles was aware, as were most naval men, of the body of opinion that considered low freeboard ships carrying normal masts and sails, to be of doubtful stability, although it was not generally thought that the *Captain* seriously lacked stability, but simply that she did belong to this suspect class of vessel.

Coles and Osborn talked long and earnestly about the nature of the

---

* The son, Sherard Cowper-Coles, invented a method of galvanizing metal known as sherardizing.

experiment embodied in the *Captain* design. They discussed diagrams and demonstrated to each other with models. Coles agreed with Osborn that if the pressure of the sails heeled a low-sided ship over beyond a certain point there was a great danger of her not recovering herself.

Osborn felt real concern for his friend's safety and warned him to be very careful to guard against serious tilting of the ship. "Don't hesitate," he said, "if you get into bad weather, to furl all sails, use steam and get her bow to the sea." Coles nodded in agreement.

There was a further meeting between the two men and Captain Burgoyne, their mutual friend, before the first cruise, and again the subject was discussed, Burgoyne agreeing entirely with the need for caution. This first cruise, however, reassured both Coles and Burgoyne about the *Captain,* for she proved to be steady and a very stiff ship: that is, it was difficult to tilt her very far under sail – she stood up well to her canvas, as sailors say.

On the night of 29 May the squadron sailed through a strong gale with a long heavy sea. James May recalled: "I was on deck several times during the night watching the behaviour of the ship in her first gale. Each time I went up Captain Burgoyne might be seen somewhere on deck in his usual working monkey jacket. This jacket, the age of which was not known, was always a signal for work, and few, if any, knew better how to get work done than he. He could exercise a peculiar influence over his officers and men. One could not possibly help working hard for him, and neither was he backward in putting his own shoulder to the wheel when occasion demanded."

May had several conversations with Burgoyne that night about the behaviour of the ship. Burgoyne asked the Gunner what he thought of her.

May said: "I think she is perfectly safe and if she weathers this gale she will weather anything." And weather it she did.

A Press observer described her as "a very good sea boat and remarkably steady – in fact, in this respect she fully equals the steadiest of the ironclads. The peculiarity of the low deck was also fully tested, as the water occasionally washed over it, wetting the deck completely, but never to such an extent as to interfere with firing the turret guns with ease and precision.

"So far the *Monarch* has had an apparent superiority of speed under sail, owing most probably to the fact that the twin screws of the *Captain,* from some cause not yet ascertained, do not revolve, although disconnected, whilst the large single screw of the *Monarch* did: but on one occasion when the *Monarch* screw ceased revolving the *Captain* excelled her in speed."

66

The explanation of this incident is that, when sailing, the screws were intended to revolve freely at the press of the water caused by the ship's motion under sail. So long as the screws were free to move they would offer little hindrance to the forward motion of the ship; but if they jammed for any reason they would act like huge brakes, or sea-anchors, offering considerable resistance to the vessel's movement.

The official report on the two ships by Vice-Admiral Sir Thomas Symonds, commanding the Channel Fleet, commented favourably on both ships regarding their ability to fire their guns accurately in any weather during which an action was likely to be fought. But he strongly criticised them both as sailing ships on account of the trouble with their propellers.

Sir Spencer Robinson, Controller of the Navy, had also been on the first part of the cruise and he added a more favourable report than Symonds, whom he thought had been unreasonably harsh in his comments. This conflict of opinion made another trial all the more desirable, although there would undoubtedly have had to be further test cruises in any case.

But this first trip to sea in the *Captain* gave Coles much greater confidence in the stability of the ship under sail, and he even spoke of her being able to outsail any ship in the Fleet.

Captain made her second cruise, alone this time, to Vigo and back between 6 July and 27 July 1870. Coles, who was on board again, asked the Admiralty if he could also accompany her on her third cruise the following month to look for further ways to improve her sailing qualities.

The *Captain* sailed again on 4 August with a squadron under Vice-Admiral Sir Hastings Yelverton, to join the Mediterranean Fleet, commanded by Admiral Sir Alexander Milne, at Gibraltar. Trials were to take place on both outward and homeward voyages.

Sail was used as much as possible and one day, according to one of Coles's last letters, "with a rattling breeze two points abaft the beam, the *Captain* and the *Hercules* (one of the fastest ships under sail in the Fleet) were ordered to disconnect screws and try rate of sailing. The ships were quickly under royals, all sail and port studding sails. They appeared to fly away from the rest of the squadron and would soon have been out of sight – although the squadron was pressing on all sail – had not the recall been made."

Coles was tremendously enthusiastic now about his ship and he almost certainly thought she was as safe as any vessel in the Fleet. "It was a neck and neck race," he wrote, "and I was delighted at the performance of the *Captain*, proving that a ship with twin screws can sail . . . I think it will be found that Sir Hastings Yelverton and all will give her credit for the character she has sustained of a cruiser under sail alone, performing evolutions and keeping station without steam, and showing that Sir Thomas Symonds was rather premature in his conclusions that ships like the *Captain* would not cruise in company with a fleet under sail alone."

Coles, on board the *Captain* was now in something like the state of excitement of a boy with a new toy. He was naturally a man of gay spirits, despite somewhat poor health due to his weak chest. He enjoyed nothing more when at home than to romp with any or all of his ten children, "seeming," as a friend said, "to be the youngest and merriest of them all."

One morning during this third cruise Coles invited May to take champagne with him in the wardroom. May was not quite sure what the celebration was for until Coles asked him if he knew the ship's position.

"Not exactly," replied May.

"We are now off Cape St Vincent," said Coles, "and not far from the spot where Nelson, in command of the old *Captain* of 74 guns, engaged and captured two of the enemy's ships at the same time. I am commemorating the event in the new *Captain*, which is able to sweep the seas."

As the cruise continued, with the *Captain* apparently confirming her qualities with each day that passed, Coles's satisfaction increased. He was not alone in his happiness either, for there was throughout the ship a very high morale and pride among the crew in having been selected to serve in such a unique and successful vessel.

Coles, although 51 and not robust, could not resist joining in the excitement of shifting topsails one night, but as he released the burton, or tackle, securing the maintopsail he got his leg trapped in it and was flung against the bridge. He described the incident in a letter, adding, "the doctor tells me I had a narrow escape from losing my leg, and so it would appear from the colour of it now, as it is black, raw and yellow from the knee down to the heel, and when I do move I hop about like a crow on one leg."

But if Coles was delighted with the *Captain*, his enthusiasm, communicated in his letters to Captain Sherard Osborn, was not shared by his old friend who was unimpressed by Coles's description of the race between the *Captain* and the *Hercules*. Osborn replied deploring the importance Coles attached to the value of a mass of sails, masts and rigging which Osborn considered "useless to her as a fighting ship, lessening her speed under steam, and which, in the event of her being dismasted in action, or a gale, might endanger the ship." Osborn told Coles that he entirely agreed with Admiral Symonds, that a turret ship should be a fighting ship pure and simple, without any masts or sails.

Yet the *Captain*'s performance under the command of Sir Alexander Milne seemed to prove Osborn wrong. She was well tested under sail. According to one observer: "A target was thrown overboard, and with all fires out and imagining the engines to be disabled, the *Captain* was worked round the target, keeping up a continual fire from her 25-ton guns.

"Although carrying an enormous load of armour and armament, she tacked under sail on a circle round a supposed antagonist, delivering irresistible broadsides of 600-pounder shot or shell. She covers her battery of guns and clears her enemy's decks at the same time by the continuous fire from the breech loaders of her small-arms men. . . . It is perfectly just to all concerned to mention that the *Monarch* turret ship could not be fought in this way in a circle under canvas alone. . . . The *Captain* goes into action on five minutes' notice, with sails furled, and steaming against a strong head sea at full boiler power. The *Monarch* required a much longer notice to clear for action and, when ready for action, is incapable of steaming against a strong head sea without the risk of putting her bows right under water and carrying away her masts."

Part of the reason for the *Monarch*'s slower time in clearing for action was that she had detachable bulwarks which carried the ship's side up higher than the main deck, affording protection against wind and weather and light shot for those on deck, and also giving some increase of stability. But the bulwarks had to be taken down to give the guns a clear field of fire.

The *Captain* also incorporated another invention of Captain Coles – tripod masts. Instead of carrying a mass of shrouds and other rigging right down to the deck's edge, where in a turret ship it would also interfere with the fire of the guns, Coles substituted three iron tubes forming a strong and fairly unobtrusive tripod brace for each mast. The tripod mast was used extensively in the French navy, but not very much in Britain, where the idea was born.

The reduced rigging on each side of the masts enabled the square sails to be braced round farther towards a fore and aft position, with some advantage when tacking and sailing closer to the wind's direction. It also meant offering greater resistance to the force of the wind, causing a ship to tilt more. This might also have contributed to the *Captain*'s foundering.

Reed had retained the traditional rigging in the *Monarch*, and this too, had to be partly removed before an action. It all took valuable – and possibly vital – time in action.

CHAPTER 10

THE ANGLE OF DOOM

One of the findings of the court martial on the *Captain* disaster was that the ship did not possess a "proper amount of stability." This finding came in for some criticism from the Board of Admiralty because it was regarded as being too vague. Their Lordships expressed surprise at the use of the words "proper amount of stability" without a full explanation of what was meant. But it is conceivable that some members of the court were not entirely clear about the precise meaning of this part of their verdict.

There had been confusion for a long time over the exact meaning of the word "stability" as applied to ships. There were experienced seamen who thought that lack of stability caused severe rolling at sea; whereas almost the complete opposite was the case. The confusion arose from regarding a ship that did not roll much as being stable – a synonym for steady – and therefore one that did roll as lacking stability.

But stability, in the naval scientific sense, means the built-in power of a ship to return to a vertical position after some force has inclined it from that position. It has less to do with a ship's reluctance to tilt from an even keel, or the stiffness of a ship, as sailors call it. In fact, the greater the angle through which a vessel may tilt, or roll, and still recover herself, the greater is her stability.

But there were many people more than a century ago who thought that excessive rolling was a sign that a vessel was dangerously top heavy. When armour-plated ships were introduced in the middle of the 19th century, and were often found to roll heavily, they were criticized as being top-heavy with armour.

Frequently it was found that lowering the weight in the hull – lowering the ship's centre of gravity – made no difference to the rolling: and yet by raising the weight – raising the centre of gravity – a great reduction in rolling was brought about.

It was all most confusing to the Victorian layman; but that did not prevent his advancing inexpert theories and criticisms in Press and Parliament. Since it was the time of great change from wood to iron hulls, and of growing dominance of steam over sail, it was new to nearly everyone; and everyone felt free to express opinions.

In Merchant Navy circles, however, it had long been observed that ships rolled more when heavily loaded with low-stowed cargo – iron rails, for example. The rolling did not mean that the vessel was unstable in the naval scientific sense; quite the reverse, for it would be almost impossible for such a ship to capsize. It would be like the once popular little toy man of childhood days who would not lie down – because he had a lead weight in his feet.

Why, then, did ships with great stability roll and less stable vessels behave more steadily under certain conditions at sea? If a ship with good stability is forced over to one side in calm water and then is suddenly released, it will return strongly to an even keel. But it will do more than this: its fierce righting force will carry it back beyond the vertical and it will continue rolling in that direction until this momentum is exhausted. Since it will then be inclined on the opposite side, the reverse righting force takes over and swings it back to the vertical and over again towards its first inclination; then it swings to and fro through diminishing arcs until it comes to rest in a vertical position – in a state of equilibrium.

In a sailing ship, movement from the vertical position is naturally caused by pressure of wind upon the sails. But at sea the forces of waves too, have to be considered. If a wave causes one side of a ship to be immersed more than the other this brings into action the same righting forces that operate when the ship is heeled, and so is irregularly immersed, by the wind pressing against the sails.

The more fiercely a ship tends to return to the vertical when tilted in calm water (i.e. the more stability it has), the more it will roll when meeting waves that pass it from side to side, or beam on, and irregularly immerse its hull. A stable ship always tries to stay *at right-angles to the water surface*; the more stability it has the quicker it tries to do this as wave surfaces change.

A ship with less stability will not roll so much – because it does not react so strongly and create such righting forces when heeled over – but, for reasons to be explained, it is more likely to be upset by sudden increases in pressure, whether of wind or wave.

A simple explanation, in part, of a ship's rolling may be seen in a pendulum. A certain force is needed to move a heavy, long-armed pendulum through 180 degrees – a semi-circle, say from the 3 o'clock position to the 9 o'clock point – and, once moving, it will continue to swing from side to side, gradually consuming the energy put into it when first moved, until it finally comes to rest.

But if the pendulum arm be short, even though the weight be the same,

71

less energy is required to swing it through the same arc, because the weight, being on a shorter arm, offers less leverage against the force, or weight, moving it. The height and distance which the pendulum weight has to be moved is obviously less than in the case of the longer pendulum: and because less energy is required to swing a short-armed pendulum to a given position, this lesser energy is therefore the more rapidly used up as it swings to and fro; and so the short pendulum comes to rest sooner than a long-armed one. It is simply a question of how much energy there is to be consumed and what it is being expended on.

As a ship rolls from side to side it may be imagined to be moving about a certain point in its hull, a point which may be likened to that from which the arm of a pendulum swings. This theoretical pivoting point in a ship is known to naval architects as the metacentre and, according to whether the ship's centre of gravity is well below, or close to the metacentre (i.e. whether there is a long or short pendulum), so the leverage exerted by the hull to bring the ship back to the vertical position will be greater or lesser.

Taking a simple floating form, a cylinder, for illustration, it will be seen from the diagram that if a weight G, representing the centre of gravity, is positioned at varying distances from the metacentre, M, then varying leverages tending to bring G back exactly below M will be exerted if the cylinder is moved out of this position of equilibrium and is then released: the 'pendulum' is being shortened or lengthened.

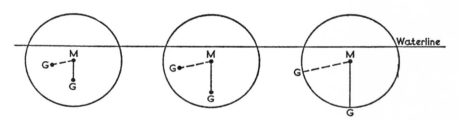

The mechanics of stability in a floating cylinder are therefore simple. But in a ship, with its less simple outline and an infinite variation of weights and their distribution throughout the hull, its reactions when disturbed from an upright position are more complex. Other pressures and forces have to be taken into account. The upward force of buoyancy must be considered.

In the case of the cylinder, because of its regular shape, the buoyancy, which acts centrally upon an object, is always pressing upwards through the centre of the cylinder and does no more than maintain its floating position: it has no part in the righting powers connected with stability which have been described. But once depart from the simple round form of the cylinder to that of the underwater section of a ship's hull, and the force of buoyancy plays an important part in the stability or righting force.

But first, to consider buoyancy: a ship, or anything else, floats because its total weight is equal to the weight of the volume of water that it displaces. The weight of water displaced, as it tries to reoccupy the space taken over by the ship's hull, causes an even pressure around the hull as it tries to lift the submerged part of the vessel: the ship is weighed against the weight of water pressing around it and is supported by it – like evenly balanced scales support one another.

So there are two forces at work: the weight of the ship pressing downwards, and the weight of the displaced water causing an upward pressure. When a ship is on an even keel the force of gravity is pressing it downwards through the centre of the hull. The force of buoyancy is pressing upwards along the same line and so the two forces are directly opposed to each other. There is, therefore, no tendency for either of them to tilt the ship. There is a state of equilibrium.

But when a ship is tilted to one side these opposing pressures cease to work along the same line. As soon as there is the slightest movement away from the vertical the centre of buoyancy moves sideways in the direction of the tilt. Immediately this happens the two forces cease to cancel each other out and, instead, create a leverage between them which tries to return the vessel to a vertical position again. They become what is known in mechanics as a 'couple'.

The more a ship inclines the farther the centre of buoyancy moves away from the vessel's centre of gravity and the greater the leverage between the two forces becomes. This force is known as the 'righting lever'.

This separation of the forces comes about because as soon as a ship begins to tilt, or heel, the underwater volume of its hull ceases to be evenly distributed about the vessel's vertical centre line. Obviously, more hull is immersed on the inclined side. This means there is a greater volume and weight of water displaced by this side – and which is trying to force its way back – than on the other, less immersed side of the ship. This condition increases the farther the vessel heels. For the reason that the force of buoyancy must act *centrally* upon this greater portion, it moves sideways from its original point of effort on the ship's vertical centre line. (See figure.)

The limit to the length of the righting lever – the maximum separation of the centre of buoyancy and centre of gravity – is reached soon after the edge of the deck reaches the waterline. If the ship continues to heel

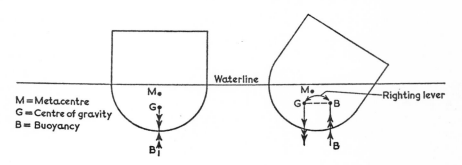

M = Metacentre
G = Centre of gravity
B = Buoyancy

Waterline

Righting lever

farther over, causing the waterline to creep across the deck, the centre of buoyancy soon begins to return towards the ship's centre. The forces of gravity and buoyancy therefore approach each other again and the righting lever shortens rapidly – and, with it, the righting force. If pressure, be it of wind or wave, or both, continues to heel the ship over, there soon comes a point at which the righting lever diminishes to nothing and the slightest additional pressure will topple the vessel over.

It will be seen from this that the height of the freeboard, i.e. the amount of ship's side above the waterline, is an important factor in stability. The higher the freeboard the farther the ship must tilt before the edge of the deck is awash and the righting force begins to weaken.

Although the analogy is not scientifically correct, the part a ship's sides play in its stability may be likened to the rockers of a rocking chair. For high sides and great stability, i.e. the ability to recover, the analogy is a chair with long, well-curved rockers. Such a chair can be rocked through a considerable angle and is difficult to turn over. It has three positions of equilibrium, the motionless upright position and the extreme limits of the rock forward and backward where, theoretically, it can be poised, balanced between recovery and upsetting. Beyond either of these two extremes the chair has no power of recovery and topples over, either forwards or backwards.

But if we consider another rocking chair with shorter and only slightly curved rockers, different characteristics are found. This chair is more difficult to rock but, after the initial resistance, it reaches the point of no return more quickly. A similar peculiarity is displayed by a ship with low sides.

Since, as has been shown, a ship's righting force increases as it tilts so long as the side is not entirely submerged, ideally then, before the deck edge reaches the water the righting force of the vessel ought to increase to a strength sufficient to resist any wind or wave pressure that may be forcing it over at sea – plus a safety margin of recovery from additional, but temporary, severe rolls that it may have to make in order to absorb the force of fierce but short-lived gusts or wave movements.

It may be that a ship with a low side will have just as much righting force as a ship with high sides *during the first few degrees of tilt*. A ship which is difficult to force from the vertical position is called a stiff ship. But the danger in such a vessel, if it has low sides, may be that it will not have sufficient reserve of righting force at greater angles to meet emergency pressures.

If a low-sided ship tilts about seven degrees in a moderate breeze, but would bring its deck to the water's edge at say, 14 degrees – and reaches its point of maximum righting force at 21 degrees, as did the *Captain* – it means that in such conditions it would have a reserve of only 14 degrees tilt during which its righting force would increase to cope with possible squalls, waves or steadily increasing wind pressure: and 14 degrees is a quite small angle to swing through. After that it could only yield to any further increase in pressure, its resistance diminishing all the time.

Clearly, if such a ship were sailing with its gunwale awash, i.e. at around 14 degrees, as the *Captain* was on her last day afloat, it would have a mere 7 degrees in hand to cope with squalls before its righting force began to weaken.

For this reason a difference of a few feet between the height of the sides of two ships might result in one of them reaching her maximum righting force at, say, 21 degrees of tilt, like the *Captain*, and having no righting force left at all at, say, 56 degrees, where she would be precariously balanced and the slightest extra pressure of wind or wave would topple her beyond the point of no return – like the rocking chair: while the higher sided ship might have reached only half her maximum righting force at 21 degrees, not immerse her deck edge until about 40 degrees, and at 56 degrees – disaster point for the *Captain* – still have more righting force left than the low-sided ship ever had even at its best angle. This, in fact, was the difference in stability between the *Captain* and the *Monarch*.

The importance attached to rolling in naval vessels was due to the effect it had on accurate gunfire, since aiming was then almost entirely a matter of eyesight and the gunner's judgment: and when everything else has been said about the employment of warships, their fundamental purpose, before the advent of gyroscopes, rockets and missiles, was to provide a platform for gunnery at sea; and the steadier it was, the better.

A compromise has always had to be reached in warship design between what is preferable and what is practicable. Since rolling is caused by the ship's reaction to wind and wave, and for given combinations varies according to the height of the side and distribution of weights in the hull, one answer to excessive rolling would seem to be to have little or no side above the water and to let the waves wash over the decks as in a low-laden barge – or the rafts that gave Ericsson his idea for the *Monitor*. But this raised problems of keeping the sea out of hatchways and other openings, as the *Monitor*'s crew discovered, and would have meant that the guns mounted on deck would be so low that even modest-size waves would obstruct the gunners' view of an enemy.

The *Captain* was a compromise, an attempt to get the best of the two worlds of steam and sail. It was this fatal compromise of a lofty full rig of sails, with the resultant heavy heeling pressure from the wind, plus the abandonment of high sides that would have withstood the heeling forces, that doomed the ship, sooner or later, to capsize.

Captain Coles's design for the *Captain* was for a deck eight feet above the waterline. This, he considered, put the guns mounted in the turrets on deck a reasonable height above the sea for good gunnery. But, when completed, the ship proved to have only 6 feet 7 inches of freeboard, 1 foot 5 inches less than designed for: and this was even further reduced when she was heavily laden.

Although this brought the height of the guns down to the same extent, it was not considered to be a serious fault. What no one, except a few scientifically minded naval architects at the Admiralty, suspected was that this variation of 17 inches was the difference between disaster and what might have been a successful service with the Fleet for the new design of battleship.

CHAPTER 11

DEATH OF A SHIP

Admiral Sir Alexander Milne stood on the bridge of HMS *Captain* with her commander, Captain Hugh Burgoyne, V.C., and Captain Cowper Phipps Coles. It was afternoon on 6 September 1870, the doomed vessel's last day afloat, and the Admiral had been inspecting the ship all day.

The *Captain* was heeling 12 degrees to starboard and a slight swell was meeting the vessel on her starboard bow as she forged her way north-ward with the rest of the homeward-bound fleet. The starboard gunwale was level with the water and the sea washed along the edge of the deck for its whole length, striking against the aft turret to a depth of about 18 inches or two feet.

The Admiral took Captain Coles to the lee side of the bridge and pointed down at the submerged deck below them.

"I shall never get used to this, Captain Coles."

Coles nodded reassuringly.

"It's allowed for in the design, sir. I assure you there is not the slightest danger."

An expression of annoyance flickered across the Admiral's face at the suggestion that he might be alarmed. There was a trace of irritation in his reply.

"The thought of danger never entered my head, Captain Coles. But do you think this is right, with a powerful ship like this, to have the lee gunwale in the water with these sails set?"

"The water can cover four or five planks of the deck with perfect safety, sir: and even up to the foot of the bridge ladder which, as you see, is some eight feet from the deck's edge."

The Admiral turned down the corners of his mouth, his chin jutting. He grunted.

"Well, I cannot reconcile myself to this state of things, so very unusual in all my experience."

It was 5.30 p.m. and the sky was darkening to the west, threatening something worse than the fresh breeze that filled the royals at the moment. The swell was increasing. Captain Burgoyne's eyes were glancing about him all the time, taking in the set of the sails, the sound of the wind through the rigging, the feel of the deck against his feet.

Although he was entertaining the Admiral in his ship and had had no sleep the night before, his seaman's instincts were active, as always. He passed the order to heave-to, the signal already having been made to the rest of the squadron on the Admiral's behalf, and he glanced up at the masthead to watch the streaming pennant gradually swing round and point dead aft as the quartermaster brought the ship's head into the wind and the sails were braced round to offer the least resistance.

The Admiral's boat was rowed across to the *Captain* and held off in the lee of the ship. As the officers chatted on the bridge, the Admiral complimenting Burgoyne on the efficiency of his vessel, which had been thoroughly inspected during the day, Burgoyne's attention was attracted more and more to the weather and the strengthening wind.

The *Captain* was rolling slowly in the swell. Every time she dipped her lee gunwale into the sea and rose again her deck scooped up tons of water, which then cascaded back over the side as she heaved herself clear.

Gunner James May, destined at the age of 36 to be the only officer of the ship's company alive within seven hours, stood by the mainmast tripod and smiled as he watched and speculated on the interest the Admiral was showing in the ship's behaviour.

The younger officers often watched this unusual sight at sea. It had been noticed that the ship rose more slowly after dipping her gunwale, owing partly to the immense weight of water to be lifted; but no one saw any danger in it, or suspected any other reason for the sluggishness.

The officers called the regular cascade over the deck's edge 'the young falls of Niagara', and it was a ship's rule that no one was to remain on the main deck if the weather was at all bad; and the doors leading to it from the poop, forecastle and deck-house were barred every night at 9 p.m. when at sea, irrespective of the weather at the time.

Captain Burgoyne spoke to the Admiral.

"We are sorry you cannot stay for dinner, sir. But without wishing to hurry you, it may be difficult to leave the ship before long."

"You're right, of course, Captain Burgoyne."

The Admiral glanced at his staff and the party moved to the bridge ladder. Down on deck nice judgment was necessary to leap from the deck into the Admiral's boat. The extent of the *Captain*'s roll varied: sometimes she dipped her deck edge, sometimes not. Sometimes the Admiral's boat alongside was actually higher than the ship's deck.

The Admiral, mindful of his dignity, chose his moment carefully and, as the gunwale sank towards the sea again, he jumped into the boat while it was still a little below the ship's side. Strong arms steadied him as he landed amid the oarsmen.

The *Captain* reached the limit of her roll, paused, and then dragged herself clear of the sea. Before the Admiral's crew could pull away the ship shed her 'young falls of Niagara' again and the water poured over the Admiral and half swamped his boat. The crew on deck hid their grins at this rare exit of the Commander-in-Chief, who dashed the worst of the water off his clothes as his boat pulled away across the wave slopes towards the flagship.

Soon after Sir Alexander reached his ship he signalled to the squadron to take in two reefs of the topsails and to have steam ready if necessary. This was the general sailing order for the night – double reefed topsails only; topsails being the sail immediately above the mainsail, or second up from the deck.

The yards for the royals were lowered to the deck, being no longer needed. The mainsails were furled and the watch set about making everything snug for the night, as the weather continued to deteriorate. Guns and turrets were checked for secure fastenings. One thing may have been overlooked.

The *Captain* had what was called a hurricane, or flying deck. This was a platform above and clear of the turrets, and ran the length of the ship, connecting forecastle to poop. It was not as wide as the main deck, through which the turrets loomed, and its sole purpose was to provide a place from which the men could handle the ropes when under sail, and to leave the main deck clear of anything that might obstruct the fire of the guns.

On the flying deck, where there was not more than the barest space for the crew to work the sails, there were also three boats, stowed lengthwise and one inside the other, between the funnel and the foremast. It appears, and has hitherto always been accepted, that during the afternoon, as part of the general preparations for worsening weather, the boats' crews were detailed to lash and secure boats on the flying deck – boom boats, as they were called, from being stowed where spare booms and spars were kept. Just as this work was beginning the watch was piped to shorten sail as the wind quickly increased in strength.

Shortening sail took precedence over routine deck work and it was disclosed by Mr May – long after the inquiry into the ship's loss was over – that the boat lashing was never completed because the watches changed as sail was being taken in and the relief watch did not attend to the boat lashing.

But did the boats that brought survival to 18 men float free for this reason? Another, and perhaps more likely explanation that was kept secret will be discussed in a later chapter. But, for the moment HMS *Captain* is sailing steadily, as she usually did, through a breezy Atlantic evening with no thought of disaster in anyone's mind. Those off duty smoked their pipes and, as men have ever done at sea, told their tales. The ship's band played aft beneath the poop. Land could be seen in the distance to starboard – the coast of Portugal.

Gunner May made the usual night rounds with Commander Sheepshanks, the second-in-command. All departments of the ship were in order and the rounds party dismissed by the poop deck. Mr May went down the ladder towards his cabin, which was in the steerage, and handy to the aft turret. On the way he met a sub-Lieutenant, Lord Lewis Gordon, who invited him into the gun-room for a drink. May stayed talking with Gordon and other officers for about half an hour and then left for his own mess.

At 9.30 p.m. May, as was his habit, went to the upper deck to look at the weather before going to bed. As Gunner, he had no watch duty in the ship; he was able to go to bed and, if he wished, sleep through the night. To that extent his was a privileged position.

There was a strong breeze blowing as he came out on to the sloping hurricane deck. A light drizzling rain blew from side to side. Staff-Commander Grant, the Navigating Officer, turned at May's approach and nodded in greeting.

"Blowing up still," said May.

"We shall have a dirty night, May, and it'll be a bad one for me," replied Grant.

His words were prophetic, as it turned out, but the Commander was not so much sensitive of coming calamity as slightly disgruntled at the thought of a wretched night's work ahead of him.

The two men exchanged a few more remarks and then May moved away to talk to Gunner's Mate James Ellis, whose watch it was.

"Evening, Ellis."

"Evening, sir."

"Everything all right?"

"All secure, sir."

May looked down over the side of the hurricane deck to where the cylindrical shape of a turret head stood up from the otherwise clear deck below. There was a round hole in the top of the turret which was used for sighting purposes in action. It could be sealed tight with a steel cover which bolted down over it. The thought to secure these covers crossed May's mind, but the weather was not really bad enough yet and he delayed decision on it and went below to his cabin – and to bed.

80

The weather steadily worsened, the wind reached gale force and there were occasional squalls of greater velocity. The gale blew from the south-west, but the current was running against it, making a confused sea without regular rhythm – one of the most dangerous conditions a seaman could meet with. Rain increased to a downpour at 10 p.m.

Aboard the *Inconstant* in station astern of *Captain*, Captain E. D'O. D'A. Aplin and his First Lieutenant saw several seas formed into "a sort of pyramid which broke on the starboard side of the ship, wetting the First Lieutenant and myself on the bridge." The height of these seas may be judged from the fact that the bridge of the *Inconstant* was 24 feet above the waterline.

Other officers in the fleet saw heavy seas coam and break to windward – that is, hurl themselves against the strength of the gale.

Aboard the *Captain* it is likely that the officer of the watch tried his best to keep station under sail alone, since the sailing qualities of the ship were under test, and to have used steam would have been, to some extent, to lose face with others in the squadron who could manage without it.

Captain Burgoyne's night order book, for the guidance of the officer of the watch, pointed out that it redounded both to Burgoyne's credit and to the credit of each individual officer of the watch, that the ship should keep her station, as much as possible, under sail alone.

This emphasis on sail was something imposed from higher authority, although there is no doubt that the crew of the *Captain* took pride in carrying out the order. There was still an obsession with sail in the senior ranks and an attitude which indicated that a real sailor was one who could handle a square-rigged ship in all conditions of weather.

On 14 August, when the ship was 120 miles from Gibraltar on the outward voyage as part of Admiral Sir Hastings Yelverton's squadron, Captain Coles wrote in one of his last letters: "The Admiral, I am glad to see, is a great man for keeping his ships under sail, when practically it can be done with economy of fuel. Keeping the ships in their prescribed order of sailing under sail, with orders only to use steam if necessary to keep station, results in a great saving of fuel, and practice to the officers (so much wanted) in keeping station and handling their ships under sail . . ."

When the Board of Admiralty wrote to Admiral Sir Alexander Milne in the Mediterranean, advising him that Vice-Admiral Yelverton was under orders to join him at Gibraltar with eight ships, including the *Captain* and the *Monarch*, they informed him:

"The Vice-Admiral has been directed only to use steam when he may consider it desirable, care being taken that the squadron shall reach Gibraltar by the 14th August, and that the qualities of the ships be tried on the way. . . . My Lords wish to have you at liberty to take such measures as you may consider most expedient for testing the various qualities of all ships, observing that unnecessary expenditure of fuel should be avoided. As several of the ships in the squadron can lift their screws, no steam should be used by them except for evolutions, as it is expected that full-rigged ships should keep their station without having their fires constantly alight."

It is not surprising therefore that in those days, when economy was deemed a virtue in the public service, Captain Burgoyne took pride in doing his utmost to obey the orders that had been passed on to him.

The orders, of course, did not mean that he was to risk the safety of his ship to carry them out; nor did his orders override the standing Admiralty Instructions "that every necessary precaution is taken to prevent accidents from squalls or sudden gusts of wind." The commanding officer had the final discretion, as always, on how the ship should be handled. But this was a time when, in spite of the advance of steam, the measure of a seaman's professional ability was still his skill as a sailor – under sail.

Gunner James May slept soundly until midnight, when the watches changed. Marines' hammocks were slung outside the door of May's cabin and as the men clattered down from the deck, wet and cold, they talked noisily, congratulating themselves on escaping below, away from the storm. Their equipment rattled as they prepared to turn in for the night. The sounds disturbed May.

As he lay in his bunk he felt the roll of the ship and thought of the guns and their fastenings. They had been all right at 8.30, but were they now, three and a half hours later – in this weather? He got up and dressed himself over his nightshirt – flannel trousers, monkey jacket, scarf, slippers and cap.

As he said later: "Some would have turned over in bed, thanked their stars they had all night in and gone to sleep again. I was not obliged by any rule of the service to get up during the night unless sent for or when 'all hands' were called for any special duty. But it is a custom of mine when at sea to turn out at any hour I may wake, have a look round, see all is right and turn in again. I always sleep better afterwards."

Never did conscientiousness have its reward as on that night. May had no thought of danger to the ship: it was simply his precious guns that concerned him.

Another incident that was to make survival of 18 of the crew possible was taking place at about the same time as Mr May was aroused by the clatter of the changing watch. But the disaster court martial and the Victorian public were never to know about it.

One man in the first watch who was relieved and could have gone below to his hammock at midnight was Thomas Kernan, a 21-year-old ordinary seaman who had been at sea for six years. In spite of the dreadful weather he could not bring himself to go down to a lower and enclosed deck. He could not swim and he was alarmed at the behaviour of the ship. Although only a seaman and knowing little or nothing about the scientific laws of stability, he nonetheless feared that the 'tween decks might be a death trap that night. Perhaps some of the naval gossip about the ship and her low sides had stuck in his mind. How then, to save himself?

As he held on to parts of the rigging and other deck fixtures to secure himself against the slope of the wet deck and the screaming wind and rain, his eyes, peering through slitted lids, settled on the big launch, lashed to a heavy crutch, or cradle, forward on the flying deck.

At the back of his mind, in spite of his fear, he knew that he could face a court martial – very likely on several charges – for what he was about to do: but the thought of drowning below, although there was not yet a declared state of emergency in the ship, overcame any such instinctive worry about possible retribution to come.

Kernan clawed his way across the heeling deck to the launch crutch, drew his seaman's knife and slashed through the ropes that secured the launch which, for the time being, remained in its stout cradle. He then either loosened or cut the canvas cover and climbed into the launch. The launch was, in fact, stored inside a larger pinnace and within the launch itself there was stowed a smaller boat, a so-called galley or captain's gig. The stack of three boats was covered overall with canvas. No one else on deck, in the tense and dramatic situation that was now developing, noticed what Kernan was doing.

How fared the rest of the fleet as the elements gathered themselves to engulf HMS *Captain*? Most of the ships were of proven design so far as height of sides, sails, rigging and stability were concerned: they would lose their sails and rigging before coming anywhere near capsizing. Several ships lost spars and top-gallant masts as a result of not taking in these upper sails and rigging quickly enough in response to the strengthening wind.

Aboard the other and 'official' turret ship, *Monarch*, designed by the Admiralty and disparaged by Cowper Coles, Captain John Edmund Commerell, V.C., had given early orders to prepare the ship for bad weather. Sails had been taken in together with all upper yards; and steam was up.

Perhaps, while these preparations were being made, one of the *Monarch*'s officers, the comparatively elderly ship's paymaster, Joseph Martin, was having a bad dream – a strange premonition of, or mystic reaction to the tragedy, depending on the time he had the dream.

83

There is no way of knowing the time but there is no doubt about the dream. Details of it were given to the author by a descendant of the *Monarch*'s assistant surgeon to whom the paymaster confided his nightmare vision of disaster *before* it became known that the *Captain* had gone down. The circumstances will be given in more detail later.

In HMS *Captain* Mr May, beginning his earnest examination of his guns, stopped to light his lantern from the swinging lamp in the gangway. The door opposite was open to the engineers' bathroom where Engineer Baron was washing off some of the grime of the engine room.

"Hallo May," said Baron. "What are you doing knocking about at this time of night?"

May smiled: "I'm going to see that the guns are all right, have a look at the weather, as it appears to be a dirty night, and then turn in again."

"It's bed for me, thank goodness. Good night, May."

May remembered these little snatches of conversation because they were the last words he exchanged with the men concerned – possibly the last words they spoke to anyone.

Unlike the American *Monitor*, Coles's turrets on the *Captain* did not revolve upon the main deck like towers; they were actually based and turned on the deck below so that the smallest possible target was offered to an enemy above deck. Only the tops of the turrets with their protruding gun muzzles extended above the main deck.

To get from the swinging lamp to the aft turret May needed only to have walked a few paces across the lower deck to enter the turret there on the starboard side, the same side as his cabin. For some reason he crossed the deck instead to the port side and entered the turret from that direction. The ship being under sail, he also had to walk against the permanent slope of the deck to reach the port side entrance: but still he did so – and saved his life.

May could not account for his having crossed to the windward side of the deck. "It would have been less trouble and more convenient for me to get in on the lee (or starboard) side."

On such whims hang life and death: if he had gone into the turret the easier way he would almost certainly have died with the ship; he could not possibly have escaped out of the lee side of the turret, for this side plunged first beneath the sea.

Captain Burgoyne appears to have come up to the bridge a little after midnight. There had been stormy weather the previous night and Burgoyne had been on deck throughout that night. It had almost certainly been his intention to get some rest the following day but, without notice, the commander-in-chief, Admiral Sir Alexander Milne signalled next morning that he would be coming aboard to inspect the *Captain.*

Having had to attend to the admiral all day until he disembarked about 5.30 p.m. Burgoyne had probably been awake and under some stress from both the weather and the inspection for about 36 hours and it was May's impression that he turned in as soon as he conveniently could after the admiral's departure and left orders that he should be called at midnight.

In normal circumstances during bad weather Burgoyne never went to bed. He would lie down in his cabin fully dressed, ready to go on deck at a moment's notice. He invariably left orders to be called at least every four hours, and more often if necessary. But on this night, when he had very likely collapsed on to his bed, exhausted, his standing orders may have been varied.

On the bridge, an exposed place, at the height of the gale he was wearing only his short monkey jacket to withstand the wind and rain: so he could have come up in a great hurry either from being called to the bridge by the officer of the watch or from his own anxiety at the feel of the ship; no time to put on top coat and oilskins. The probability seems to be that he was called; but not until the sands of disaster had nearly run out.

No one who survived knew precisely when Captain Burgoyne took command of the situation. But, there he was, a little after midnight, in charge. Shortly before May came up from below Burgoyne called James Ellis, 29-year-old Gunner's Mate, to the bridge and told him:

"Take a man you can rely on, Ellis, and put the tops on the turret sighting holes. And come and report – to *me* mind – when you are finished."

"Aye, aye, sir."

As Ellis left the bridge and called to James Frost to help him screw on the turret covers he heard Captain Burgoyne shout:

"How much is she heeling now?"

"Eighteen degrees, sir," came the reply from the man at the pendulum roll indicator.*

Despite later argument about how much Captain Burgoyne really knew about his ship's stability, there can be no doubt that this cry above the noise of the gale meant imminent danger to him.

The Officer of the Watch called out: "Lower the topsails and then man

---

* To indicate a ship's angle of sailing, or roll, a heavy pendulum, or pointer, hung free against a scale of degrees by the bridge. As the ship tilted the scale moved accordingly behind the pendulum (which remained motionless and vertical) and so the angle of tilt could be seen at a glance.

the weather foretopsail brace." This may have been relaying an order given by Captain Burgoyne, at his side.

The ship gave a lurch and Burgoyne's voice was heard above the shipboard clamour:

"Let go the foretopsail halliards. Plenty of hands go forward and man the downhaul." And as the rush of feet drummed across the deck he yelled his further desperate orders.

"Let go the maintopsail halliards. Let go the lee topsail sheets."

The effect of these orders, if they could have been carried out in time, would have been to let the sails fly free and release the dangerous wind pressure that was steadily bearing the ship over. But it was too late. Even had a man been stationed with an axe at the bitts – the big wooden deck posts through which the sail ropes were secured – it is doubtful whether the axe blow would have cut loose the sails soon enough to save the ship. For the sea now came to the wind's aid.

One of those who rushed forward to carry out Captain Burgoyne's emergency orders was the senior rating, Captain of the Foretop Lewis Werry. He would tell the court that enquired into the disaster: "As I was making my way forward to let go the topsail sheets, I just got as far as the boom boats when I saw them floating out of their crutches."

Ordinary Seaman Thomas Kernan was, willy-nilly, already on his way clear of the doomed ship.

In the aft turret James May was bending to shake one of the gun chains: it was quite secure. But as he rattled it he felt the ship shudder under the blow of a wave. The deck tilted to an angle such as he had never known before – and went steadily farther, steeper and steeper until it became obvious that the ship would not and could not recover herself.

May dropped his lamp and leapt for the sighting hole that had been above his head a few moments before, but which was now swinging down in front of him as he braced himself back to remain upright. The hole was 22 inches in diameter – just enough for a man to struggle through. The gun muzzles, poking out of the lee side of the turret, were already under the water as May wriggled clear. The water was, in fact, level with May's escape hole, for the ship at that moment was on her side. The weight of her guns and metal masts carried her farther over now that all stability was gone.

The *Captain*'s movement from her normal sailing angle to the completely capsized position was a steady, irresistible motion. It was this smooth, inevitable progress of the ship as it turned turtle that enabled some remarkable escapes to be made.

Leading Seaman Charles Tregenna had just come on deck with the middle watch and he leapt for the foretopsail halliards at Burgoyne's

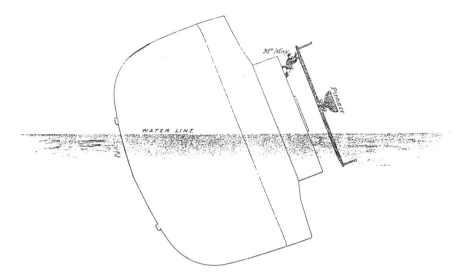

Official diagram showing how Gunner James May escaped through the hole in the top of the turret.
(*Courtesy of Ministry of Defence Archives*)

command. He loosened the halliards and tried to haul down the sail. But something was jammed: the yard would not come down.

As the ship heeled over he realized it was beyond recovery and obeyed his sailor's instinct at such times and made for the 'high side'. He clambered to the edge of the windward side of the deck as it rose higher and higher out of the water. Then he walked, bit by bit, first out along the now horizontal ship's side, and then gradually worked his way round the curve of the hull as she turned over; until at last he was standing where the keel would have been if the *Captain* had had one. The sea then washed him off. David Dryburgh, Able Seaman, also made this fantastic walk round the hull.

Gunner's Mate Ellis held on to a grating as the ship went over and the ship's launch, with Kernan aboard, bruised Ellis's back as it was washed over him as he hung on to the grating. Ellis went over with the ship, clinging to his deck grating until he was beneath the sea surface. He then let go and came up to see the launch floating 15 yards away. He struck out for it.

Others of the watch were washed off the tilting deck even as they struggled to release the sails. For the rest, below decks, the end came swiftly and in some cases horribly.

CHAPTER 12

OF WIND AND WAVE

When James May came to the surface he saw the *Captain* bottom up and sinking rapidly. Above the noise of the storm could be heard the sound of the ship's insides rending apart. Undoubtedly, the two great turrets ripped themselves out of the ship once she had turned over. They were designed to rest and operate on heavy mountings below deck; not to hang from them with the ship upside down. Their going would have left two holes each 26 feet in diameter for the sea to pour through and drown all those below deck.

Heavy machinery aboard, shot, shell, provision casks and other heavy weights would also have broken loose and added to the short-lived horror of those who awoke to experience their last brief moments.

There was a heavy explosion that was probably a boiler bursting. May said later that he heard no cries from within the ship. Other survivors spoke of screams coming from the funnel which, of course, gave direct access to the stokehold.

Whether their screams were heard or imagined, it is inconceivable that the ten or so men who were on duty in the stokehold could have faced such an end in silence. The stokeholds of the early steamships were unbearable to a landsman; and the men who toiled in them were also a class apart from the deck seamen.

A typical stokehold was a black alley, some 60 feet long and nine or ten feet wide. Situated in the lowest part of the ship, it was lit only by a high grating at deck level, walled by furnaces near floor-level, and boilers that nearly met overhead.

There would be 40 or 50 furnaces in a big ship. The floor was heaped with coal that tumbled about until the atmosphere was a fog of black dust. The heat was unendurable – except to stokers. They worked stripped to the waist and must have acquired some resistance or unusual tolerance to the awful heat blast that burst from the fires whenever a furnace door was opened.

Their labour was unceasing. With each man responsible for several

88

fires, no sooner was one glutted with coal than another white-hot mouth gaped for it.

The events below when the *Captain* reeled on to her side can be guessed with reasonable certainty. Either the boilers would have torn loose from their mountings, crushing all; or steam and boiling water would escape and the furnaces belch out their fires. Either or all of these things must have happened and turned the dark hold into a brief inferno in which no man could restrain his terror.

So the survivors who said they heard cries coming up through the ship's funnel as it dipped into the sea near them, while they struggled to reach wreckage or boats, may well not have been mistaken.

May found himself near to Captain Burgoyne in the confused sea. One of the watch on deck, Able Seaman John Heard, was also nearby. Burgoyne, who could not swim, shouted for help. As May put it afterwards: "He begged of me and John Heard to assist him to the bottom of the pinnace, which we did."

The pinnace, a steam-driven tender, had not righted itself as it should have done on entering the water. It floated bottom up and already one or two men had reached it and clambered on to sit astride the keel as best they could.

May and Heard struggled through the water, supporting Burgoyne between them and managed to get to the pinnace. They climbed out of the sea and hung on.

Meanwhile, another little drama of survival was taking place not far away. Leading Seaman Charles Tregenna, who had stood on the bottom of the *Captain* after making his way round the ship's hull, struck out for a piece of wreckage about 20 yards away as the sea lifted him clear of the sinking ship. He clung to the wreckage for a few moments, while two other men tried to hang on to him in the violent water. In their struggles they tore off Tregenna's trousers and were swept away to their deaths.

Tregenna caught sight of the launches, one inside the other, as they had been stowed on deck, but floating right way up. He abandoned his piece of wood and began swimming towards the launches. As he neared them he found himself close by Able Seaman David Dryburgh, the other hull walker. A sudden mouthful of water made Tregenna splutter and cling instinctively to Dryburgh for support.

"For God's sake let go," yelled Dryburgh. "You'll drown the pair of us."

They were close by the boats.

"Hold on while I get in."

There was a small hole in the taut wet canvas cover of the launch.

Dryburgh stuck a foot in and ripped it enough to get a grip, climbed up and pulled Tregenna aboard after him.

Tregenna had an open knife dangling from its lanyard. He had opened it when Captain Burgoyne's order to release the foretopsail sheet had come – too late. Before Tregenna had had a chance to relieve the ship with a stroke of his knife she had surrendered to the sea and all Tregenna had to do was try to save himself.

But now the open knife was invaluable. It made short work of the rest of the drum-tight canvas. Other survivors were hauled in. The launches had by now separated, the lower one sinking away, and the one holding the survivors was to windward of the upturned pinnace on which six men now clung: they were Captain Burgoyne, James May, Able Seaman John Heard, Boy 1st Class James Saunders, Ordinary Seaman Robert Tomlinson and Able Seaman William Laurence.

As they huddled there, still only a few minutes after the ship made its fatal roll, they saw the bow of the *Captain* reaching straight up above the waves as she began her plunge down.

"My God, May," said Burgoyne, "I never thought we were coming to this. Throw off your jacket and look out for this boat righting."

Contemporary engraving of the scene immediately after the *Captain* went down. (*Courtesy of Ministry of Defence Archives*)

Already resigned to his fate, the Gunner answered, shouting above the storm:

"It's no use, sir. I may as well die in my jacket as out of it. This boat will never right."

The vertical fore end of the *Captain* sank the last few feet and the stem disappeared beneath the surface.

"There she goes, sir," cried May. "And we shall soon follow her."

"I'm afraid so, May," came the reply. "This boat shows no sign of righting."

They were melancholy, hopeless exchanges, but they are the exact words used to the best of May's recollection.

There was an awesome gurgle from the sinking ship as the waves closed over her; it was heard even above the noise of the storm.

It was difficult to cling to the keel of the pinnace. Men were washed off and struggled back several times. Then, tantalizingly, it seemed that there was hope of early rescue, for, only 50 yards away to leeward, the survivors saw a large ship. It was the *Inconstant* which had been sailing astern of the *Captain.*

It was a fleeting hope, however. May described the moment in a report to the Admiralty: "We all hailed her, but I suppose the howling of the sea and wind prevented them hearing us."

Very soon the *Inconstant* was lost to sight.

But help was at hand – for a few seconds.

The launch, with Tregenna and Dryburgh and others now aboard, was moving swiftly before the wind. It bore down on the pinnace and passed it close by the stern at an angle of about 45 degrees.

May was nearest to it. He had an arm hooked through the frame in the keel which housed the propeller of the upturned boat. He hung there, much as a man might loll in a chair, with his arms hooked over the back of it. But the waves flung him about and dashed him against the sharp edges of the propeller, cutting and bruising.

The launch came close enough to touch and May, crying "Jump, men: it's your last chance," thankfully relaxed his painful handhold and leapt for the launch. Dryburgh and the others grabbed him and hauled him in. Several more followed May.

Burgoyne called out for a line to be thrown. Lewis Werry, Captain of the Foretop, who was in the launch, held out an oar. One of the men on the pinnace grabbed it and for a few seconds the two boats were linked together.

"Hold on to that oar, boy. You'll need that," cried Burgoyne to Werry.

"Jump men, jump," he urged them.

Several more seamen plunged from the pinnace into the foaming strip of sea that separated the boats, and were hauled into the launch. But Burgoyne himself made no attempt to leave the keel.

John Heard was still beside him when the pull of the launch dragged the oar from the hands of the man who had seized it. The man immediately jumped into the water and gained the comparative safety of the launch.

There were only seconds left as the gap widened. Heard, emboldened by their situation, tried to encourage Burgoyne to jump. "I'll jump with you, sir," he said.

Burgoyne shook his head.

"Jump and save yourself, lad."

The launch was already 20 feet away. Heard flung himself off the pinnace and, swimming with desperate strength, gained the launch. It swept on before the wind and within a few seconds there was nothing to be seen but the furious sea. Burgoyne was lost to sight and no man saw his end. May said later that he thought he did jump; but others did not agree.

In the launch May, as the senior and sole surviving officer, had urgent decisions to make. The open boat offered but a slender chance of survival in such weather, and that only if she were handled properly – and quickly so.

There were 19 men on board, including May. There were nine oars left in the boat. Leading Seaman Tregenna, a man of great experience, took one and used it as a steer oar in the stern to keep the launch head before the wind.

May gave his orders quickly. "Come on lads: throw all that loose tackle overboard. Keep baling, some of you."

All they had to bale with were their caps – those who still had them. While some scooped water out in this way, others heaved overboard a galley (smaller boat), iron shackles, spars and other ship's gear that had been stowed in the launch. The rest manned the oars, four a side. As soon as the boat was cleared May decided to try and find Burgoyne and any other survivors.

"Put her round, Tregenna, and see what we can pick up."

Tregenna knew all about steering small boats in heavy seas and ventured to question the order.

"If you try, sir, you'll swamp the boat in this sea. Keep her before it and we shall do."

"I said put her round," snapped May. "Captain Burgoyne's back there, and maybe others."

Tregenna argued no more and swung the stern round. The launch immediately began to lurch violently as the seas caught it broadside on. The men were flung from side to side and hung on as best they could.

There was a momentary slackening of the motion as the boat slid into the trough of a wave. Myers, at one of the oars, called out encouragingly: "Now lads, I think we are all right."

As if roused to fury by this suggestion of safety, a heavy sea broke into the launch and washed Myers out, oar as well, for his temerity. He was not seen again.

The boat was suddenly half full of water. Another such wave would mean the end for all of them. May realized that it was no use to try further to get the boat's head round into the wind.

"All right, Tregenna. Put her before the wind again."

Dryburgh, who was one of the regular crew of the launch, knew where everything was stowed and soon had a pump rigged. Meanwhile baling continued with caps and anything that would hold more than a handful of water.

May knew that the coast of Portugal lay to leeward, or dead ahead as the wind drove them, so he was content to concentrate on keeping the launch seaworthy and let the wind take them where it would. He had little choice anyway.

There was seldom more than a few yards visibility. Sometimes the launch wallowed in a valley of the waves with a watery hill both astern and ahead. At such times the boat lost way and was virtually becalmed in the hollow. The men who strained at the oars had a sight of the following sea rolling towards them, roaring and threatening to over-whelm them. At such moments May's cry would summon fresh efforts from their aching arms.

"Pull for your lives, lads."

The oars forced the boat away from the following sea. Movement was vital to give Tregenna a chance to keep the boat end on to the wind. Without way on, his steer oar was virtually useless.

Then, as the sea lifted them, the launch would be held like a surfboard on the crest of a wave. The men had a sensation of flying with the wind. They were thrilling, fearful moments – for there was constant danger at such times that the boat might swing across wind and wave and be capsized or swamped.

The thought of relieving Tregenna crossed May's mind; but the horny-handed Cornishman said he was all right and seemed to be tireless. May knew that nobody else aboard could handle a boat as well in such weather and was thankful that the problem needed no more of his attention.

About 1 a.m. the squalls became more frequent, with heavy wind-whipped rain. Some of the men found it difficult to hold on to their oars against the snatch of the wind. Several were torn from weary hands and literally blew away, flying through the air like pieces of straw.

May, sitting in the stern, grasping the gunwale, cried out: "Hold on, lads. We'll be lost without oars."

At times they had to hand oars from one side of the boat to the other to cope with sudden swings which were too much for the oars on one side to counter.

For a long time three of the crew were no use in the struggle for survival. Two boys, James Saunders, aged 17, and John Gribble, 17, lay in the wet bottom of the boat in a state of complete exhaustion and shock. May, occupied though he was with everyone's survival, spared an occasional glance for the two still figures and wondered whether they would live or die before the night was out.

Petty Officer Lewis Werry was also very ill. Heavily clothed, and wearing a tarpaulin coat over all, he had gone down with the ship in its first roll and had swallowed a great deal of water. He was barely conscious when hauled into the boat. Although he had held out an oar to those on the pinnace, it was with the last shreds of his consciousness and strength, sustained by the peril of the moment. He was placed next to David Dryburgh, who worked tirelessly at the pump.

Werry recovered a little with the warmth of Dryburgh's body and the rhythmic movement as he worked the pump. Soon Werry put a hand to the pump himself. It was feeble assistance, but the exercise gradually improved his condition.

It was two hours before May found time actually to count the number of men in the boat. Very little was said, and what it was necessary to say had to be shouted above the gale which blew undiminished for three hours after the disaster. The men simply pulled at the oars, baled or pumped, each knowing that to relax might settle the fate of them all.

About 3 a.m. the weather showed signs of improving. The clouds that had made the night so dark, broke up. The wind still blew very hard; but now, the stars could be seen.

May looked up, saw the North Star to the left and knew that they must be heading approximately for Cape Finisterre, almost due east. For a while now the moon came out and a little feeling of hope seeped through the men as its light spread over them.

The weather was clearer to the east and they caught an occasional glimpse of a light as the boat rose to the tops of the waves. As soon as the first cry of 'Light ahead' was raised, every eye that could turn in that direction peered as each wave peak was reached to see whether it was Finisterre or the masthead light of some vessel. May decided that it was the Finisterre light.

No sooner had he come to this conclusion than several men saw another light about 400 yards to windward – over their stern, to the west. This was probably HMS *Bristol,* one of the fleet.

According to May: "She was then on the starboard tack under fore and aft canvas and apparently with steam up. Some of the men suggested that we should try and close her to get on board, but I thought it the wisest plan to continue our course before the wind and sea, fearing to turn the boat's head to windward after losing Myers the way we did."

As he shook his head at the suggestion there came a cry: "She's seen us."

All eyes were on the dark mass of the ship. She was coming round. Both bow lights were visible for a few seconds to the 18 men in the boat. But she did not run down to them. Her sails were hauled to the wind and she lay over, heading northwards with the wind on her port side. She was soon lost to sight.

CHAPTER 13

LANDFALL IN SPAIN

The men bent to their oars again. Gradually the wind moderated and for a short time became quite light. It seemed that their troubles were nearly over. But hardly had relief begun to spread through the survivors than the wind shifted suddenly to the north-west, blowing hard again from that direction.

The sea became more confused as a heavy swell from the south-west clashed with the north-west wind. The sea broke wildly and unexpectedly in the darkness. The men not rowing baled for their lives and were hard-pressed to keep pace with the repeated swampings which the boat received. They pulled on through the night, performing the motions of rowing with the mechanical numbness that eventually sets in when men drive themselves beyond their normal limits of physical endurance.

May watched the eastern sky ahead of him gradually turn pale grey and then glow faintly somewhere beyond the sea as the first gilded harbingers of dawn appeared on the horizon. A new day came: a day that only a few hours earlier they had had little hope of seeing. A new day, new hope: and as the light improved, May saw Cape Finisterre dead ahead.

The weather improved as the sun rose higher. The gale slunk away until the only trace of it was the long heavy swell from the south-west which helped the boat on its way towards the shore.

In the fresh early light the land seemed to be about four miles away, and May discussed it with the men in whom the sun had put fresh life. Two hours' steady pull was the general estimate of the time they would need to reach land: but as the sun climbed higher the land seemed to get farther away. It was, in fact, more than four miles off; distances are deceptive at sea just before sunrise and just after sunset.

If any were disappointed it was no more than a passing thought. A pleasant breeze was now blowing and May would have given much for a sail to lighten the labour of the men at the oars. They tried various makeshift sails. They split up two boat covers and laced them together with rope yarns. The improvised sail was then spread out between two boarding pikes: it helped a little.

Other pieces of canvas were cut up to make caps, as only three of the men in the boat had retained hats, and those who were bare-headed were beginning to feel the heat of the sun. Ellis suggested that they ought also to cut canvas to cover their feet, for those without shoes would need something to walk on when they reached land. May thought it was a good idea; and, at least, it occupied those not rowing now that there was no longer any danger of the boat's foundering.

As the morning warmth increased they began to get thirsty, for with the exception of one man, Thomas Kernan, they had all been in the sea and swallowed varying amounts of salt water before reaching the launch.

During the morning there were a few heavy showers of rain. It was tantalizing to see so much fresh water about them but they had nothing in which to trap it. It is a curious fact that the idea of spreading the boat cover that they were using as a sail to catch a supply of rainwater did not occur to anyone. Or, if it did, it was not tried otherwise May must surely have recorded the fact. The men simply turned their faces to the sky and opened their mouths wide, savouring the few drops of rain that they managed to catch in this way.

It was nearly midday when they pulled past Cape Finisterre, against which the waves were dashing to a great height. What the lighthouse-keeper made of the open boat that came in from the sea can only be imagined; but he hoisted the Spanish flag as the survivors pulled past the Cape.

The shore was still difficult to pick out in detail and, as they coasted gently along the south side of the Cape, they saw what appeared to be the roofs of houses in the distance. Several of the men pointed eagerly, but May was doubtful about it, as he could see no chimney smoke above them.

He was also reluctant to keep to the course they were steering, since it would take them head-on to a lee shore with which he was completely unfamiliar. With the breeze dead behind them and a sea running, this was a dangerous thing to do because, if the shore turned out to be rocky and impossible to land upon, they would find it difficult, if not impossible, to pull away and prevent the boat being driven ashore if they went in too close.

May's doubts about the roofs were confirmed a few minutes later as, with a change in the light, they were revealed as rocks to which a trick of sunlight had lent a roof-like appearance. They continued pulling south, parallel with the shore, until they reached the centre of Corcubion Bay. Soon, on the port side, they glimpsed the top of a red-tiled building which proved to be the village church of Finisterre.

They turned east again, heading for the shore, and soon the whole village came into sight. As they approached the beach, a boat with two men in it came out to meet them and piloted them to a snug little cove between two big rocks, where they were able to beach the boat easily.

There was a chorus of "Thank God" from the men as the bows crunched aground. Twelve hours had passed since the *Captain* sank. A man who spoke English of a kind told May that he was Captain of the Port and took charge of the survivors. The boat was hauled up and stripped of everything movable. Spanish women gathered round the exhausted Englishmen and broke into tears at their sorry state. Some brought them food and wine.

May's duty began to press upon him as soon as he set foot ashore. It was his responsibility to get news of the loss of the ship to the Admiralty as soon as possible.

"Where is the British Consul?" he asked, in the deliberate tones of the Englishman abroad.

The Captain of the Port smiled reassuringly, and said there was one at Corcubion and the *señor* should see him at one o'clock. At one o'clock he promised that the Consul should appear at two o'clock; and at two o'clock he was equally reassuring to the *señor* about the prospects for three o'clock. May was uneasy and did not trust the man. Somehow he had to get a letter or telegram off to England.

During this delay a drunken Spaniard, apparently overflowing with goodwill, had pressed upon May a dry shirt and cap, for which he was grateful, although preoccupied with his problem. Not content to rely any longer on the Captain of the Port, he found another Spaniard and a Spanish policeman who offered to show the way to Corcubion which, they said, was about three miles away.

May gathered his men together and they set off, barefooted for the most part. As the motley party trudged out of Finisterre the drunken Spaniard lurched up to May, snatched the cap off his head and rudely demanded the return of his shirt. Although a chilly September evening was approaching, and May was left with nothing but a pair of trousers, he did not argue but gave the man his shirt.

The men were about to lay hands on the Spaniard when May ordered them back. He was a mild and simple man who, recalling the incident, said: "I did not feel the insult, my mind at the time being occupied with other and deeper reflections: and soon afterwards I got another shirt from someone who was fortunate enough to possess two. Our guides also lent me a jacket and cap."

The way led them across the beach of Corcubion Bay and past a fish-curing shed. The curer came out as they passed and advised them to go no farther that evening as the roads were very bad. He offered them shelter for the night. No doubt a fish-curing shed would not have been the ideal place to spend a night, but May had other reasons for not wanting to waste time.

"No, thanks," he said. "We must get on."

The various descriptions they had heard of the road ahead were not exaggerated – "almost as rough as the sea we had traversed during the night" was May's own description of it. The going became worse as darkness set in and May began to consider whether they should have to sleep out in the rough scrub country which surrounded them.

He was able to put this thought from his mind when a bright moon appeared over the hills and showed the way clearly. But it seemed a long three miles, even taking into account the roughness of the road and their lack of footwear. From time to time May tried to find out from their guides how much farther they had to go.

"Corcubion?" he would ask, gesturing ahead. But as neither of the two Spaniards could speak a word of English they merely grinned reassuringly and replied, "*Si, si* . . . Corcubion" – which did not add to May's knowledge of their situation.

Nearly all the survivors had cut and bruised feet. James Freeman, an ordinary seaman, dashed his foot against a stone in the darkness and broke a toe. May's feet were also in a bad way. They had, in fact, walked and hobbled about six miles when the guides motioned them to halt in the middle of a village. They were all hoping this was Corcubion; but it was not. The guides had simply thought it a good idea for everyone to drink some water. May took the opportunity to bathe his battered feet.

After this brief halt they marched on again. As the party moved away one of the guides signalled to May to remain behind. He kept repeating something, but May could not understand a word. However, glad of an excuse for a few minutes further rest, he sat where he was. Two of the men, Laurence and Harvey, stayed with him.

There was a considerable delay during which May began to wonder whether he was right to waste so much time, but eventually one of the guides appeared with a saddled mule which, he indicated, was for May to ride. May was no horseman but anything was better than the brutal footpath; and he managed to stay in the saddle.

He offered the mule to Laurence and Harvey on the way, but they would not trust themselves to the saddle, preferring their own tortured feet.

At last, late at night, they reached Corcubion. They had walked, not the three miles forecast but just on ten. The irony of the painful march was that they could have reached Corcubion easily in their boat, in their own element.

On inquiry, May found that the British Consul was away for the night; but a courier was dispatched to the Consul at Corunna with news of the disaster. Local officials looked after the survivors, providing clothes, food and lodgings for the night. After seeing that the men were all right May at last went to the room provided for him. He sat down.

His own recollection of the night is: "In this quiet solitude I began to realize most keenly all that had happened and the terrible scenes I had passed through during the previous 20 hours. Yet it was difficult to understand it all, for it seemed to me more like a dream than reality, that our fine ship had gone down into the fathomless deep, literally swallowed up with her splendid crew of 500 souls. I was very tired and laid down to rest; but sleep was out of the question. If I dozed off my rest was disturbed by hideous dreams and so great was the effect produced on my mind that for several nights and days I could not get any sound sleep, my whole nervous system suffering very much."

Next morning, 8 September 1870, the British Vice-Consul returned to Corcubion and sent to Finisterre for the survivors' boat and belongings which had been left there. May began his first official report on the loss of the ship.

"To the Secretary of the Admiralty", he wrote. "Sir, it is with great regret that I have to report to their Lordships the total loss of Her Majesty's Ship *Captain*, which occurred about 12.15 a.m. of the 7th, the ship at the time being under double-reefed fore and main topsails, on the port tack, close-hauled with the wind about north-west, very squally with rain and a heavy sea . . ." (May was incorrect about the direction of the wind, which was approximately south-west according to the logs of other ships in the fleet.)

Briefly describing his own escape, he concluded: "I think it possible that there may be more survivors in some of the other boats. We are all under the care of the Vice-Consul, in good health, but some are very much bruised. The boats of Her Majesty's Ship *Monarch* have just arrived under the command of Lieutenant Arundel to take us on board that ship. I hope soon to be in England to give a more detailed account of this melancholy catastrophe."

May was mistaken in thinking there might be other survivors. He and his 17 men were all who remained alive. It was perhaps ironic that cutters from the *Monarch*, E. J. Reed's ship and the *Captain's* rival should have brought the rescue party into Corcubion and made first contact with the survivors.

Although May described Lieutenant Arundel as being in command of the search party – and perhaps technically he had been given that command – Captain Edmund Commerell of the *Monarch* and his assistant ship's surgeon Charles F. K. Murray, had also gone ashore with the party and joined in the search on foot and by mule along the coast until they found the survivors at Corcubion.

The survivors poured out their stories to the officers and fellow sailors. One of them, Thomas Kernan, told his story to Dr Murray and perhaps to Captain Commerell at the same time, but that is less certain. What he said, in the boundless relief of rescue, was to remain a secret, for reasons that can only be conjectured, for more than a century and will be discussed in the context of the *Captain* court martial that was to follow.

The weather was too bad to put to sea again that night but on the morning of the 9th, the Vice-Consul having arranged for the dispatch of May's report, the survivors sailed in the *Monarch*'s two cutters and made rendezvous with *Monarch* and *Volage* off Cape Finisterre.

On the morning after the disaster HMS *Psyche*, steaming up from Vigo, came across grim evidence of the *Captain*'s loss, although her crew were not immediately sure which ship had gone down. But floating on the still-troubled surface of the sea they saw the body of Seaman Hart, clinging to a grating without any lashing: death had not prised his rope-hardened fingers loose from the grating that had offered him a desperate hope of survival.

During the day several of the *Captain*'s boats were also come upon, including the larger launch in which the survivors' boat had been stowed, and which floated away water-logged moments before the first men hauled themselves into the launch that was to save 18 lives. The water-logged bottom launch was picked up by HMS *Bellerophon* and taken to England.

A variety of other flotsam from the *Captain* was also picked up by the fleet: it included the hurricane deck, part of the *Captain*'s bowsprit with a sailor's long silk scarf tied to it, several flags, the top-gallant yards and the binnacle. Towards evening a piece of panelling painted ebony and gold was found: it had come from Captain Burgoyne's cabin. The hurricane deck is believed to have been torn off by the guns and turrets as they fell out of the capsized vessel.

Meanwhile, as May and the other survivors sailed homewards in the *Volage*, a stunned country waited for further news. For the first few days the Admiralty received scores of telegrams from anxious relatives to whom only the bare news could be replied: one officer and 17 men are safe.

Joy was brought to a few homes on 9 September by a telegram from Gibraltar reporting that some of the *Captain*'s crew had been transferred to other ships before she sailed with the Fleet.

101

"The *Captain*, before parting company from the *Prince Consort*, discharged into her: W. Wingate, W. Bund, T. Hogarty, James Moore, Alexander Smith, Thomas Wise, Henry Williams (A.B.'s); James Page, Corporal of Marines, and W. Taylor, Midshipman, discharged to *Royal Oak.*"

On 10 September a poignant telegram arrived from Lieutenant Rawson, of Western Cottage, West Street, Bude, Cornwall, on behalf of Mrs Burgoyne, wife of the captain of the lost ship. Addressed to Sir Sydney Dacres, First Sea Lord, it read: "Mrs Burgoyne has given up all hope, but she wishes me to ask if you would kindly telegraph the slightest item of news. She is calm and very quiet."

But there was no more news to come – of anyone.

Grief is not graduated according to class or social position and if officers are singled out for mention among the lost it is because more written information exists in the families they came from.

Thus it is known from family papers that 15-year-old Midshipman Edward Ryder, a kinsman of the then Earl of Harrowby and of Rear-Admiral Alfred Ryder, died on what would probably have been his last voyage even if the disaster had not occurred. He suffered from a family weakness, short-sightedness and had had to give up signals training for this reason: it was becoming more and more embarrassing for him to carry on with his naval career and he would almost certainly have left the sea if the *Captain* had reached England again.

The loss of Midshipman Childers, son of the First Lord of the Admiralty, is worth separate reference because of the self-reproach that must have troubled the First Lord's mind.

His was the political responsibility for carrying through the building of the ship, although it had been authorized during a previous administration; that was the chance of politics. But his grief was sharpened by the fact that he had used his influence to get his midshipman son transferred from the *Monarch* to the *Captain* after her first successful trials, when she was being popularly acclaimed as the finest ship afloat.

Possibly he may have taken some satisfaction, owing to his disagreement with Reed over future shipbuilding policy, in removing his son from the 'unsatisfactory' official turret ship. But Fate seldom deals a father such a cruel blow in time of peace.

CHAPTER 14

THE COURT MARTIAL

The court martial ordered to try Gunner James May and the 17 survivors assembled on board HMS *Duke of Wellington* in Portsmouth harbour, on Tuesday, 27 September 1870. It was an event for which the whole country had been waiting and the Press were there in force. Admiral Sir James Hope, Commander-in-Chief, Portsmouth, was President of the Court, which was so to upset the Admiralty and Parliament by its findings.

It began with Sir James reading out the formal convening order from the Admiralty:

"Whereas Admiral Sir Alexander Milne has reported to us the loss of Her Majesty's Ship *Captain* on the 7th day of September 1870 and whereas we thought fit that a court martial shall be held pursuant to the custom of the Navy to inquire into the loss of the said ship, and that Mr James May, Gunner 2nd Class, and the surviving petty officers of the said ship shall be tried under the 91st and 92nd sections of the Naval Discipline Act, 1866, we do hereby require and direct you to assemble a court martial as soon as conveniently may be, which court (you being President thereof) is hereby required and directed to enquire into the cause of the loss of Her Majesty's Ship *Captain* and to try the said Mr James May, the surviving petty officers and crew of the said ship accordingly."

It may fall a little harshly upon civilian ears that, having gone through the ordeal they had, Mr May and the others were now to be put on trial. In fact, it was not a trial in the generally understood sense of the word. It is certain, however, that if the facts had disclosed that either May or his men had behaved in a cowardly, negligent or unseamanlike manner at the time of the disaster, there would have been some retribution. It will be considered at a later stage whether this consequence was deliberately avoided. But this court martial was more in the nature of an inquest into the death of a ship and, incidentally, some 500 men.

Nevertheless, Mr May's sword lay across the table, lengthwise in the traditionally neutral position for the time being. Not until the court had reached a verdict would its position be changed – point towards Mr May if he were found guilty, hilt towards him if he were judged innocent.

It was a formidable court which included officers who had commanded other vessels in the fleet the night the *Captain* went down. In addition to Admiral Sir James Hope, there were Vice-Admiral Sir Hastings Yelverton, and Captains George Hancock, Edward Rice, Henry Boys, Charles H. May, John Edmund Commerell, Thomas Brandreth and James G. Goodenough.

The early evidence dealt with the individual stories of the survivors, beginning with Mr May's original report, written in the room at Corcubion, Spain, the day after the disaster. It told in brief graphic phrases of the loss of his ship. A second statement by May, giving slightly more detail of the events, was also read.

The President then addressed May:

"Have you any complaint to make against any of the surviving crew?"

"None whatever."

"And have you other survivors anything to object to in the statements just read to the court or anything to lay to the charge of any officer or man with reference to their conduct on the occasion of the loss of Her Majesty's Ship *Captain*?"

"No, nothing," murmured the seamen in reply to this comprehensive question covering improper conduct of any kind.

The President then began the first of days of questioning of scores of witnesses, questions all aimed at trying to discover the reason for the disaster. Had it been due to bad seamanship or an inherent fault in the design of the ship?

The President: "Have you anything further which you wish to add to your statement, already read to the court, which would be calculated to throw light on the loss of the *Captain*?"

A heavy responsibility rested upon May as the only surviving officer, and a man whose intelligence had been proved by his advancement through the ranks in the service. His was an opinion that would be considered of great importance. He chose his words carefully:

"I think the over-pressure of canvas, and the ship making a very heavy roll to starboard, brought a body of water on the lee side of the main deck. Possibly the wind may have acted on the underside of the hurricane deck, and the sea most likely struck her when she made the heavy roll, and she might have been in a peculiar position with regard to the crest of the wave. All this tending to capsize the ship."

"Have you ever seen the ship roll heavily?" asked the President.

"The greatest roll I ever knew her to make was about 14 degrees."

104

"Both ways?"

"One way."

"How much the other way?"

"Probably not more than one or two degrees."*

"During the course of your service in the *Captain* did anything occur which gave rise to a suspicion in your mind of a want of due stability in the ship?"

"Nothing," replied May. "I always felt myself in the finest ship in the world until she foundered."

The other members of the court were invited to ask questions and Vice-Admiral Sir Hastings Yelverton probed the practical point of whether the *Captain* was designed so that its crew could work well and easily.

"Do you believe that the hurricane deck afforded ample room for working the ship?"

"No. When the hands were on deck it was very much crowded."

"Do you believe the topsail sheets were well placed for letting go when they were secure?"

"No. They were belayed over the fore and main bitts."

"From your experience of the *Captain* did it strike you that she would not be safe if she got into a heavy squall, without the power of shortening sail?"

"No. I should have thought the topmasts would have carried away before the ship capsized."

"Do you think the arrangement of ropes on the hurricane deck was such as to admit of shortening sail if suddenly caught in a squall?"

"We were rather cramped for room."

They were simple, direct answers to searching questions by experts. If a seaman of May's experience conceded that the men were "rather cramped" when working on the narrow platform above the main deck, then it is likely that conditions there in an emergency of ship and weather were against bringing swift relief to the stricken vessel.

Captain Rice tried to clarify the exact circumstances of the ship's turning over.

"Did you feel the ship hove over by a sea?"

"To the best of my belief I did."

"You, of course, understand the difference between a ship hove over by a heavy sea and the feeling of a ship pressed over by her sails? Your feeling was that the ship was hove over by a sea as well as pressed by her canvas?"

---

* Pressure of wind upon the sails would prevent a full roll to windward.

"Yes. She made a heavy roll and did not recover from that roll, and it is my impression that a sea struck her bilge and helped her over."

May concluded his evidence with a tribute to the way the men had behaved, and in particular Charles Tregenna, who had steered the launch.

Petty officers, seamen and boys, the rest of the survivors, each told their personal stories of escape, including the fantastic survival of David Dryburgh, A.B. . . . ". . . gradually as the ship turned over I walked over the ship's bottom. Finally I stood upon the bilge piece, the seas closing over me. I came up to the surface; then I saw the launches, one inside the other, and struck out for them."

Captain of the Foretop Lewis Werry told of the last moments of Burgoyne and two seamen who remained on the upturned pinnace and failed to reach the launch. One of the men was named Scivens, he thought, but he could not identify the other.

The President asked: "Do you consider Captain Burgoyne failed to jump for the launch from being exhausted?"

"No," replied Werry. "I believe Captain Burgoyne would not leave that boat while the other two men were on her."

"What grounds have you for supposing that Captain Burgoyne would not leave the pinnace until he saw the other two men safe?"

"Because I heard him tell them to jump."

It seemed, from the evidence of James Ellis, the Gunner's Mate, that the first watch had gone below before the middle watch were all on deck for the formal relief; but this was not particularly unusual if not strictly according to regulations.

"Had the watch finished mustering when the order was given to let go the topsail halliards and sheets?" came the question.

"No. Captain Burgoyne gave orders for the watch, as they mustered, to man the weather foretopsail brace and downhaul. The watch was about half-mustered when the order was given to let go the foretopsail halliards."

The picture of what happened that night was emerging clearly enough; but the court's task was to try and find out why it happened. Several officers of other ships in the fleet, while agreeing that the weather had been very bad, were unanimous in their opinion that their own ships were never in the slightest danger, nor did they feel any alarm.

The 30th witness to be called was Lieutenant Ernest Rice, who had been with the Controller of the Navy, Vice-Admiral Sir Spencer Robinson, aboard the *Monarch* during the first trial cruise with the *Captain* the previous May. Rice had made a report to the Controller on observations he had made during the cruise.

The President quoted from it: "The *Captain* did not appear to rise to the seas as quickly as the *Monarch* and on the 11th and 12 of May a great deal of water washed over her main deck and against the turret. The *Captain* had the appearance of an overloaded ship. The *Captain* is not a ship which should be pressed under sail. A heel of 14 degrees would bring her gunwale to the water and from that point, of course, her stability would very rapidly decrease."

"Now, Mr Rice, is that extract from your report to the Controller?"

"Yes, it is."

"State to the court your opinion of the circumstances which occasioned the foundering of the *Captain.*"

Rice was not a naval architect, nor had he more book learning about ships than the average naval officer of his time. He thought it right to make that clear.

"I would first respectfully state to the court that the opinion given in Sir Spencer Robinson's report was founded upon what I thought to be my practical experience as a seaman and not upon theoretical knowledge. And I gave that opinion taking three things into consideration: first, the low freeboard of the *Captain*; secondly, the size of her masts and spars; and thirdly, combined with these two, what I knew of the distribution of her weights during the trials."

"State to the court in what respect you consider the low freeboard of the *Captain* affected her stability."

"Up to the point of the gunwale of the ship being brought to the waterline, the pressure of water against the submerging side of the ship would act against the force by which the ship was being heeled over. But once the water came over the edge and on to the deck the resistance would be removed and her stability would rapidly decrease if she continued to heel over."

"Did you ever state to Captain Burgoyne that you considered the ship unsafe when pressed to a certain point?"

"I believe I did."

"To the best of your recollection did he agree with your opinion?"

"Captain Burgoyne was a very old friend of mine and to the best of my recollection he made a joke of it."

Lieutenant Rice concluded his evidence.

There was a natural reluctance by the members of the court to throw doubt on the judgment and seamanship of a dead colleague, particularly one such as Burgoyne, whose career had been so gallant and distinguished: and withal he had been a popular personality. Several witnesses had already been asked whether sail had been taken in on their own ships, a question which, in the circumstances, tended to cast

107

doubt on the wisdom of the *Captain*'s carrying the sails she did.

But a miscalculation as to how much sail a ship could safely carry in bad weather usually resulted only in torn canvas. Seamen brought up in the old world of high-sided ships seldom had to worry about the possibility of their vessels actually turning upside down.

The court now knew, although it had not yet been formally elicited in evidence, that the *Captain* was a dangerous vessel if allowed to heel over too far in conditions where she might be subjected to a further sudden

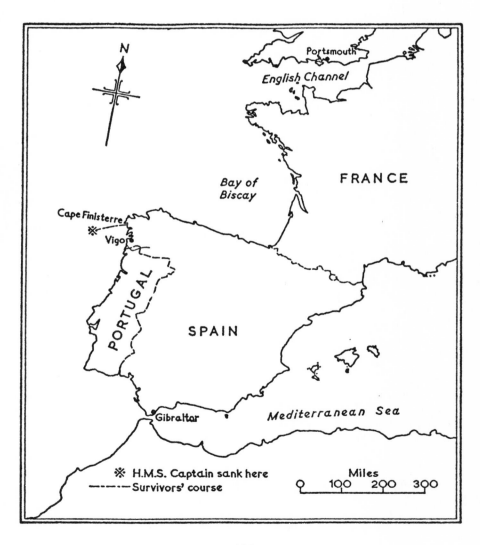

※ H.M.S. Captain sank here
------ Survivors' course

lurch by wind or wave. This was now common knowledge in naval circles. But the point to be established was, did Captain Burgoyne know of this inherent danger in his ship as a fact?

Admiral Sir Alexander Milne, who commanded the fleet during the *Captain's* last voyage, was called.

He told the court that when he took command of the combined squadron he received special instructions from the Admiralty to report on the capabilities of the *Monarch* and the *Captain*. Dealing with his inspection of the *Captain* during her last day afloat, the Admiral said: "I had some discussion with Captain Burgoyne about the way the sails were set and he said it was Captain Coles's idea. Captain Coles gave me his opinions and I did not pursue the matter.

"During the trials the ship was heeling about 12½ degrees and I observed on several occasions that the heel was rather over 14 degrees. There was no special lurch; she just slowly and quietly recovered herself back to 12 degrees."

Referring to his disquiet about the sea's washing along the lee side of the main deck while the ship was under sail, and his brief conversation with Coles on the subject, Admiral Milne said: "As it was my intention to have again visited the ship I did not enter further into the matter."

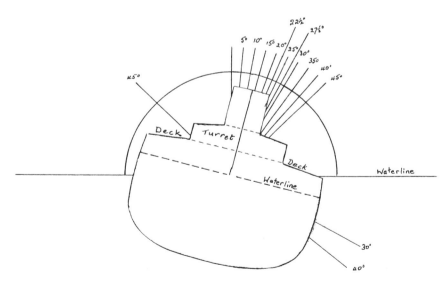

Official diagram of the *Captain's* hull when she was heeling 14 degrees in a modest sailing breeze and the deck had reached the waterline.
(*Courtesy of Ministry of Defence Archives*)

"Was the weather on the night of September 6th such as to cause you any anxiety for the safety of any ship of the fleet?" asked the President.

"None whatever," came the reply. Every time this question was asked in some form or other – and it was put many times – the fact that the ship was at fault and not some freak of weather became more apparent.

The President: "It has been given in evidence that when the squalls struck the *Captain,* causing her to founder, she was under double-reefed topsails and, as I think, foretopmast staysail. Do you consider that that was fit sail for such a ship to have been under in such weather, observing that by 'such a ship' I mean a ship – an experimental ship – the seaworthy qualities of which had not been ascertained?"

This was a slightly difficult question for the Admiral. Was there any suggestion in it that he ought to have issued special orders to the commander of the *Captain?* His reply was non-committal:

"I should have thought that Captain Burgoyne, or the officer of the watch, would have lowered the topsails to the squall, but I think the topsails would have torn away before any such ship should have gone over."

"Do I understand you to mean by that answer that if the *Captain* had possessed the proper stability for a ship of that size, the topsails would have blown away before she could reach the point at which she would capsize?"

"I think so."

The President tried another approach.

"Can you give the court any opinion as to whether the *Captain* would have been safe during that squall if her square sails had been furled and she had been placed under steam instead?"

"She would probably have been more safe under steam."

It was a safe reply, too, and did not take the enquiry much further.

"The opinion I wish to elicit from you," the President persisted, "and which is very important to the proper conduct of our present enquiry, is whether, if the ship had been handled as I have described, she would now have been afloat or not – observing that, however anxious the court must necessarily be to obtain your opinion on that point, there is no desire to press it if you are disinclined to give them the advantage of it."

The Admiral now had the unpleasant task of trying to answer without unduly criticizing a distinguished dead officer, or of being wise after the event. He did not succeed, although he no doubt spoke honestly.

"I have every inclination to give my opinion to the court but that ship was in the hands of an able and experienced seaman. He had steam at his command to do whatever he considered best for the safety of the ship. If I had been in command, it is very probable that I should have furled sails and used steam. But in the case of the *Captain,* commanded as she was, I cannot say what were Captain Burgoyne's views and feelings on this occasion."

"Will you describe to the court to what you consider the actual foundering of the *Captain* was due?"

"I think she must have heeled over beyond the angle that I saw when on board, and most probably some portion of her lee deck was under water; and also, at the same time, she was struck by a heavy sea to windward and thrown over."

Here was a repetition of Mr May's evidence, but with the additional weight of a Flag Officer's rank behind it. The Admiral stood down.

Officers from other ships in the fleet that night were called and asked about the weather, the amount of sail they were carrying and whether they had any doubts about the safety of their ships in the prevailing conditions. Without exception they confirmed the view of the Admiral, that although it was a rough night, there was no danger. But several ships had reduced sail more than had been considered necessary on the *Captain.*

Captain Thomas Brandreth, a member of the court and captain of the flagship HMS *Lord Warden,* in which Sir Alexander Milne flew his flag, was called as a witness. He said he had been on the deck of his ship at 20 minutes past midnight, at which time the *Captain* went down, and he described the weather.

"We had what I consider a severe squall. The topsails had been lowered before 12. That squall split the foresail and the fore-topmast staysail. The sea was confused but not heavy. It did not become heavy, as stated in the log, until 1.30 or 1.45, when the squalls, I think, were heavier."

"From your experience as a seaman, and such means of observation as you had of the *Captain,* do you consider that it was either right or prudent to have been carrying on under double-reefed topsails when the squall struck her?"

"No. I should have endeavoured to shorten sail, as it is stated that Captain Burgoyne did."

Thus was Captain Brandreth able to say what he would have done without actually criticizing a fellow officer; for it was not clear whether Burgoyne had been on deck and in charge before the squall struck, or whether he had come up and, too late, tried to do something that the officer of the watch ought to have done earlier, inhibited though he might have been by Burgoyne's night orders. Brandreth said he thought if sails had been furled and the ship had used steam only the *Captain* would have come through the night safely. He was not being wise after the event because the topsails of the flagship had been lowered before midnight by his own orders.

111

"Do you know if any other ship than the *Captain* carried her topsails hoisted through the squalls from 12 to 12.30?" asked Captain Hancock.

"As far as I can gather, no," said Brandreth.

The impression was being created and reinforced with each expert witness that the *Captain* had been carrying somewhat more sail than was prudent in the circumstances. But even if this were so and pride in the new vessel had impelled its officers to dare the wind, in a ship of its size the sails ought to have ripped away before they could sustain sufficient wind pressure to drive the ship right over.

Since, with the exception of May, who, as Gunner, would not have taken much part in conversation with the navigating officers, all the officers were dead, the court had to rely upon recollection of what they had said at various times to throw light on what they thought of their ship.

Captain Rice asked Brandreth: "After the ships had been made snug for the night, was it usual to make signal to the fleet to reef in squally weather, or was it left to the discretion of the captains?"

"It would depend on the state of the night: if the fleet had been in sight and the Admiral had contemplated reducing sail permanently, the signal would have been made."

"The signal was not made on the occasion in consequence of the ships not being in sight – and therefore useless?"

"Yes. There was no ship in sight at the time of the squall, and the only one in sight afterwards apparently had her topsails close reefed."

"Before the squall came down suddenly a little before 12, were there any such indications of approaching bad weather as would have made it in your opinion, necessary to signal the fleet to reef?"

This was a question Brandreth could not have answered in the affirmative without challenging the judgment of Sir Alexander Milne, whose failure to signal he would have been criticizing. His reply was quite definite.

"Certainly not. At 10.30, when the fleet were in sight, I considered the ships were under easy sail for the night – but possibly might have to shorten sail or reef."

"Do you mean that you thought it might be necessary to signal or that ships, finding the weather getting bad, might possibly think it necessary to reef?"

"I thought it might be necessary to reef," replied Brandreth, "as I left word in my own orders: but I did not contemplate a signal."

"Then the flagship would have reefed without making a signal even had the fleet been in sight"

This was still a question which suggested that some responsibility for the *Captain*'s failure to shorten sail – and survive the night – might be laid on the flagship and the Admiral.

"She would have commenced reefing directly it was necessary," came Brandreth's textbook reply, "but would probably have made a signal while doing so."

This line of questioning was possibly more for the record than to reveal any significant information to the court. Of course, all members of the court, being of the rank of captain or above, had had years of sailing with fleets and knew perfectly well what the normal procedure was at sea in company with other ships.

"From your experience of fleet sailing," Captain Rice persisted, "is it customary or not to look to the flagship for directions as to reefing, as long as she can be seen?"

"Yes, usually."

There was a faint possibility that had not yet been explored that the *Captain* had experienced a freak gust, entirely local to her position, and not experienced by any other ship.

Captain Boys asked: "Do you think it probable that the *Captain* had a different force of wind in the squall at 12.20 from the *Lord Warden*, to which she was next in line?"

"I think she must have felt the 12.20 squall as much as we did," said Brandreth.

A witness whose short evidence threw some light on why the officer of the watch had risked so much sail in bad weather, was Commander C. N. Hoare, who had been Flag Lieutenant to Sir Alexander Milne during the cruise and inspection. As one of the Admiral's staff he had naturally talked with the officers of the *Captain* and had generally kept his eyes and ears open.

He said that the general impression he got was that the *Captain* was "heavily masted, that the hurricane deck was rather limited for general work, that the ship was very steady." With these few reservations, and the fact that the *Captain* was not much good beating to windward, Hoare found that the ship's officers were all confident in the vessel and her sea-going qualities.

"Had you any conversation with any officer who kept watch in the ship as to the orders they received from their captain relative to the management of the ship, or as to carrying sail?" asked the President.

"No," replied Hoare, "but I did see the Captain's night order book, and so became acquainted with the orders left at night-time for the guidance of the officer of the watch."

"State what those orders were."

"All the orders I saw tended to impress upon the officer of the watch that it redounded both to Captain Burgoyne's credit and to the credit of each individual officer of the watch that the ship should be kept in her station, as much as possible, under sail. If however, during the night, she should drop out of station they were particularly required to use every effort at daylight to be in their station, and he referred to the good name the ship had obtained for keeping station."

There it was: a significant pointer to what in an ordinary ship with high sides might have been a somewhat reckless disregard for the safety of Her Majesty's sails, but which no one realized, in the case of the *Captain*, was gambling with the fate of the ship herself.

CHAPTER 15

SAILORS MUST SAIL

An important expert witness was Mr W. B. Robinson, Master Shipwright and Engineer of the Royal Dockyard, Portsmouth. Robinson had been in charge of the fitting out of the ship before she sailed on her first cruise on 10 May 1870. He was someone whom the court could question about the technical evidence with which they had been supplied by the Admiralty.

One of the documents supplied to the court was a diagram showing the varying stability, or resistance to being pushed over, that the *Captain* had at various angles. It was called a curve of stability.

Referring to this, the President said: "I find the angle at which the deck would be immersed to be 14 degrees, and the angle of maximum stability to be six more, which is 20 degrees, and that she loses her stability altogether when she is inclined at an angle of 40 degrees. Do you consider a ship with only the stability described to be a fit ship to send to sea under sail?"

"Yes," replied Robinson, "if properly masted and handled."

"Are you sufficiently acquainted with the masting of the *Captain* to be able to offer an opinion as to whether she was overmasted or not?"

"I have no exact knowledge of the facts regarding her masts and sails, but from the little I know accurately of the elements of the ship, I am of opinion that she was overmasted and made too much like a regular sailing ship."

Robinson said he could not recommend the style of masting for a ship like the *Captain* without knowing all the details of her construction, but he agreed that any such recommendation would have to take into account the ship's righting force and the pressure on the sails – depending on their area – at different wind strengths.

"And you would propose leaving a sufficient margin for an accidental increase of wind, or the force of the sea operating to turn her over?"

"Yes."

The President now turned to the question of the ship's centre of

115

gravity and other theoretical calculations related to its stability and seaworthiness.

"Are you of opinion that all these calculations, which involved the safety of the ship, should be most carefully made by her constructors before they commenced to build her?"

"Yes, certainly."

"Might such calculations be safely disregarded with ships resembling one-another in great measure?"

"If they were such as had been previously constructed."

"But would you not consider it highly culpable not to have made them most carefully in the case of a ship entirely new in form and size?"

This was a most flagrant leading question, but the ordinary rules of examining witnesses do not appear to have been observed in this instance.

Robinson replied: "Some might be disregarded in ships of very similar type and nearly of the same dimensions, but under other circumstances on no account should the calculations be disregarded."

This was a clear criticism of Lairds, if not of Captain Coles.

"Are you able to state whether these calculations are invariably made in the construction department of the Admiralty?"

At this point Captain Blake, the Judge Advocate, stepped in as guardian of the Civil Service and reminded Robinson that as a government official he need not answer any question if he thought doing so would be prejudicial to the public service.

To have replied 'Yes' would have made the Constructor's department appear to be beyond reproach – and might not have been true either: to have said 'No' would have suggested that Lairds' assumption of some aspects of the design was no more than common practice and something that was just as usual in Admiralty establishments. Robinson's reply shed no light upon Admiralty dockyard working customs of that time.

"Officially, I am not informed on that point," he said.

"Would you be satisfied, as a naval architect, to build a ship which, if she lurched 40 degrees, would upset?"

"No, not if she lurched 40 degrees without sail on her."

"Are you aware that it is not uncommon for line-of-battle ships to lurch considerably more than that without the slightest danger?"

"I had in mind low freeboard ships, comparatively. I am aware that a high ship might lurch to that extent without danger."

"Would you be satisfied to send a low freeboard ship to sea, as a steamer only, without masts, if her condition of stability were such that she would be in danger of turning bottom up if she lurched nearly 40 degrees?"

"No," replied Robinson.

This was an important answer, because the facts of the *Captain's* stability were known shortly after the ship sailed for the third and last time; and nobody had thought it necessary to send a message to Captain Burgoyne, or the Commander-in-Chief, or to question the wisdom of sending her to sea complete with a full rig of sails and heavy masts.

Captain Boys: "What would, in your opinion, be the consequence if, under sail, the *Captain* heeled suddenly to a squall as much as 30 degrees?"

"That would depend upon the permanent angle of heel she was at while sailing."

"Supposing the permanent angle to be 30 degrees?"

"She would go over without doubt."

The President asked Robinson whether the experiment of inclining a ship forcibly to find out the position of her centre of gravity was done because the calculations that were made could not be absolutely relied upon, or was it done simply to test them?

Robinson said that the calculated position of the centre of gravity in a new design was necessarily approximate, and that therefore Admiralty designers would naturally verify their calculations by this experiment.

The President: "It has been described to us in evidence that when the

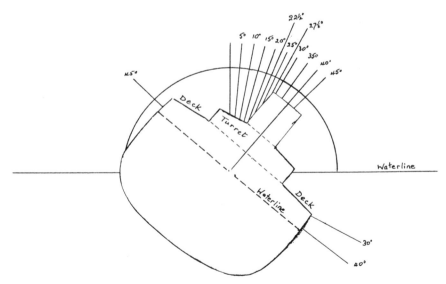

Official diagram of the *Captain's* hull when she was heeling 40 degrees and would soon reach the point of no return.
(*Courtesy of Ministry of Defence Archives*)

117

Captain turned over, the turning motion appeared to be continuous. That is to say, she made no stop whatever, either when her masts were lying horizontal, or at any other time. May that be considered as a practical proof that she had passed maximum point of stability at a comparatively small angle of inclination?"

"It would appear to indicate that."

"A well-conditioned ship, in point of stability, with her hatches well battened down may be thrown on her beam ends by the pressure of sail, or the violence of the sea, but when relieved of the weight of her masts, by their carrying away, the pressure of the wind being off the sails, she might then be expected to right – this being something of which we have repeated instances. Is that a view you would take of the case?"

"Yes – of a high freeboard ship."

Captain John Edmund Commerell, V.C., who commanded the *Monarch*, told the court of "frequent conversations I had with Captain Burgoyne and Captain Coles respecting the sea-worthiness of the *Captain*. Two days after arriving at Vigo, Captain Coles, in the presence of Captain Burgoyne, who did not dissent from it, expressed to me his greatest possible confidence in the stability of the *Captain*, and said that beyond a certain point she could not go over. Captain Coles altogether laughed at the suspicion of her capsizing. I had reason to believe from conversations which were very frequent that Captain Burgoyne had thought the ship overweighted, but, from the recent trials, his mind was perfectly set at rest upon that point."

This was the fatal deceptiveness of the ship. Although the Admiralty experts had misgivings about her stability, and practical seamen thought her overmasted and therefore top-heavy, the fact remained that, notwithstanding theories and appearances, the ship had proved at sea to be very steady and heeled only to a limited extent – even though the edge of the deck soon reached the water because of her low sides.

Referring to the night of the disaster, Commerell said: "I saw the *Captain* up to 11 o'clock and she appeared to me just as usual, not heeling over or labouring in any degree, and when morning dawned and she was absent I had not the slightest anxiety for her safety."

Commerell added that he had, in fact, been anxious about the ship after a storm on the previous 30 May, during her first cruise – the one that had reassured Gunner May as to the *Captain*'s seaworthiness.

The question of Captain Burgoyne's seamanship – or that of his officers – was brought up again.

The President: "Do you consider, viewing the state of the weather shortly previously to the time at which the *Captain* was lost, it was either right or prudent for Captain Burgoyne to be carrying his double-reefed topsails when the squall struck the ship at about 12.20?"

Captain Commerell answered: "I know now, and have no doubt in my own mind, that double-reefed topsails were too much sail for the *Captain* to carry. I presume that he was holding on to reef with both watches the moment the middle watch had been mustered. The weather had been very changeable, but no doubt the squall was very heavy."

"Were you on deck between 12 and 12.20 on the morning of the 7th?"

"I was. I came on deck at 11.25. The squall was then threatening and at 11.40 I ordered the fore and main topsails to be lowered: not on account of the force of the wind so much as because I had no spare topsail yard, and I did not like to run the risk of springing one. At the moment of lowering, the maintopsail split and the wind gradually increased."

"If the *Captain*'s sails had been furled and she had been placed under steam, is it your opinion that she would not have foundered?"

"It is: but I do not consider that the weather was such as to warrant the *Captain* working out of line. She had weathered storm in safety, and therefore I consider Captain Burgoyne would not have been justified in breaking out of line."

This answer shows why Burgoyne had been so keen not to use steam if it could be avoided, and why either he or his officer of the watch had been keeping as much sail aloft as possible to maintain position in the fleet and demonstrate that they and their ship could sail as well as the rest. Captain Commerell, for one, would clearly not have thought much of Burgoyne if he had broken station that night.

"Why do you consider placing the ship under steam necessarily involved hauling out of line?" asked the President.

"I do not think he could have furled his topsails with the wind abeam. If his topsails had been aback* the ship would have gathered sternway. It happened to me twice on that night – and that only caused by my main-topsail being aback to save the sail."

"Why should the ship have gathered sternway with an unlimited power of using steam?"

"Before two o'clock, going ahead with three boilers, with the foretop-sail split and the maintopsail aback, my ship went astern at the rate of at least two knots; so much so that I thought a mistake had been made and the engines had gone astern."

This graphic reply showed the force of wind and current that the fleet had to contend with that night. But the *Captain* had certain other diffi-culties as well.

---

* Aback – sail caught awkwardly by the wind and blown in reverse direction against the mast, so that a ship may be driven backwards in certain conditions.

"Was the *Captain* so short-handed as to seamen as to make it desirable to have both watches on deck in getting her topsails in?"

"I think so. She had 25 men less in complement than I have, with the same sails and spars, and heavier gear, and more unhandy leads to her ropes."

Captain Rice put a variation of the same line of questioning: "Considering the reputation of the *Captain*, then, for stability and seaworthiness, do you think that two double-reefed topsails and a foretopmast staysail was an imprudent amount of sail with respect to the safety of the ship, up to the time at which we are informed Captain Burgoyne attempted to take them in?"

"I do not think so. I should have done it myself if I had wanted the assistance of both watches to reef."

"If you had known the calculated state of the stability of the *Captain* and had commanded that ship, would you have considered it proper to carry square sails at night at all, except in the finest and most settled weather?"

Again, it was a leading question that left no doubt in the mind of the witness as to the answer expected. On this point, at least, these two members of the court were in absolute agreement.

"No," replied Captain Commerell. "Not without reference to higher authority."

The court now turned to the emergency arrangements aboard the *Captain* for taking in sail. Several of the survivors were recalled and asked particularly whether hands were stationed by the topsail sheets and halliards (sail control ropes), and whether they knew where the boatswain's axes were kept.

The significance of this question was that in an emergency, when sails might have to be released quickly to relieve the ship of wind pressure, the only way to do it in an instant was to slice through the ropes that held the sails to the wind with an axe or knife.

There were no specific Admiralty orders that men should be on duty for this purpose but, as always, there was a standing Admiralty instruction that officers should take care that their ships were not endangered from squalls or sudden gusts of wind. This put the onus on individual commanders or officers of the watch to take whatever action they thought right to safeguard a ship in the particular circumstances of wind and weather.

It appeared that no hands were stationed by the ropes, ready to cut them loose, on the night of the disaster. But this only meant that no one in authority on board foresaw the possibility of desperate measures having to be taken to save the ship.

120

The *Captain*'s sails were not cut free in time because the order, when it came, came too late. It will be recalled that Captain Burgoyne was heard to call out for "Plenty of hands go forward and man the downhaul . . ." and, a few moments later, "Let go the foretopsail sheets . . . let go the foretopsail halliards." But, of course, by that time the ship was already beyond the point of no return.

The next witness, Captain James Goodenough, also a member of the court, gave strong support to the amount of sail that was carried on the *Captain*.

"My opinion on the cause of the *Captain* foundering has necessarily been influenced by her fate and the evidence which I have heard," he said, "but my opinion before her loss, and when I was in possession only of the information concerning the ship which the officers of the squadron in general possessed – and I believe all that the Vice-Admiral in command possessed – was that the *Captain* could have carried her double-reefed topsails and foresail in entire safety through the night of her loss."

The President: "Did you consider the weather at any time during the night in question was such that a captain, believing in the seaworthiness of his ship, would have been justified in hauling out of line?"

"No," replied Goodenough.

CHAPTER 16

AGAINST ALL THE EVIDENCE

Interest quickened as Nathaniel Barnaby, President of the Council of Construction, took his place to give evidence. Barnaby had been one of E. J. Reed's principal assistants and had only been in his position as President of the Council of Construction a few weeks. This council was formed after Reed's resignation. The appointment of Chief Constructor was not filled for the time being and the Council was set up with joint responsibility for the duties previously carried out by Reed.

Barnaby told the court that Lairds had applied to the Admiralty for the centre of gravity of the *Captain* to be ascertained, by inclining the vessel, on 24 February 1870 and that the ship was actually inclined on 29 July.

"Why did this delay take place?" asked the President.

"The reason for the delay is partly explained in their Lordships' reply of 26 February to Messrs Lairds' letter, in which they said: 'Steps shall be taken to ascertain the vertical height of the *Captain*'s centre of gravity when an opportunity offers, and the weather is settled, but it is not considered desirable to attempt to carry out the experiment before the forthcoming steam trials are completed, or while the weather is unsettled.'"

"Will you explain to the court in what way the forthcoming steam trials affected the question?"

"It would have been necessary that the ship should have been brought into the steam basin, that she should have remained there till a calm day could be found; and this delay in making the steam trials, in order to ascertain whether the speed of the ship was in accordance with the contract, was considered by the Chief Constructor and their Lordships to be inadvisable."

"What are the facts as to the ship's stability, as calculated subsequently to the 29th July, the day the ship was inclined?"

"The centre of gravity of the ship was found to be situated at a depth below the water of nearly three feet – actually 2.9 feet – and the distance between that centre and the metacentre was ascertained to be 2.6 feet."

This was a vital fact, proved in evidence for the first time. The figure

2.6 feet was the length of the *Captain*'s theoretical pendulum on which the 'bottom' weight of the vessel hung and swung and tended to restore the ship to vertical whenever it became tilted. The longer the 'pendulum', the greater the anti-roll force exerted by the ship's weight as she tilted (see Chapter 10) or, more simply, the greater her stability.

"Was the captain of the ship informed of these facts?" asked the President.

"Calculations were not completed, and we did not ourselves know the position of the centre of gravity until 23rd August, the ship having left on her third and last cruise on 4th August. When that calculation was complete we saw nothing in it to cause us to apprehend, in the face of the reports of the officers who had tried the ship at sea, that she was in danger of capsizing."

This was the tragedy of the matter. These calculations were highly theoretical and not understood by any except naval architects and, as was later disclosed, had even been challenged as to their value by one eminent naval architect. So to have questioned the stability of the ship on the grounds of a theory not universally accepted, and in defiance of the practical experience already gained in the ship at sea, would have been difficult for the Constructor's Department, who might have found themselves accused of blackguarding the *Captain* because it had been built against their advice but yet had proved to be a good vessel.

"From the evidence and from various reports of the sailing trials of the *Captain* which have been published," said the President, "it would appear that not only Captain Coles and the officers of the ship, but also the Flag Officers who made these reports, were entirely unconscious of the dangerous want of stability of the *Captain*, as shown in the diagram – where I observe that the maximum amount of stability is only 20 degrees and that at 40 degrees it vanishes altogether. Under these circumstances would it not have been desirable to have placed the officers I have mentioned in possession of the information with the very least possible delay?"

Barnaby explained that the diagram was prepared to show the stability of the *Captain* in the event of her higher bow and stern portions being so damaged that they would give no assistance in stability. While the ship was undamaged the stability was somewhat better than shown and the righting force would not vanish until the ship was inclined to 54½ degrees.

The court left that point for the moment.

"Can you give a comparison between the stability and righting force of the *Captain* and the stability and righting force of other well-known ships?"

Barnaby explained: "For angles of heel up to the immersion of the *Captain*'s gunwale the stability of the *Captain* would not differ very materially from that of the *Monarch*. The difference is that the high side of the *Monarch* caused her stability to be twice as great at 28 degrees as it is at 14 degrees; whereas in the *Captain* the stability at 28 degrees was very little in excess of what it was at 14 degrees.

"As a matter of fact, we have no ships with which to compare the *Captain*. She was an experimental ship designed with a low freeboard, and it was well known that one of the advantages of a low freeboard was that the angles of rolling as compared with the angles of rolling of ordinary ships was very small. Captain Coles always urged this and instanced the case of the American monitors whose angle of roll did not exceed six or seven degrees. It was impossible to foretell to what extent the *Captain* would have this same advantage.

"The Controller of the Navy considered the experiment a dangerous one, although it was not possible to tell to what extent it might be so. No one supposed it would be perilous, or involve the loss of the ship. I myself was the first person to point out the element of danger introduced by putting sail upon such ships."

The court sat absorbed as this comparatively unknown civil servant told in matter-of-fact terms of the important discoveries he had made about ship design. Barnaby had carried out the first investigation made into the stability factors involved when putting masts on low-sided ships.

"These first calculations were completed on 7th September 1867," he went on. "They were not made with any reference to the *Captain*, they were made by me in preparing an answer to a proposal made to cut down some of our two-decked ships, put turrets in them and mast them. The freeboard proposed for these ships was three feet six inches – at least, that was the estimated height of freeboard.

"In my report I said, then having in mind the *Captain*, 'This element of danger requires to be borne carefully in mind in all turret ships carrying sail;' but as no one has hitherto proposed to have less than twice the amount of freeboard now advocated, the exact amount has never been calculated before.

"My view of the case was adopted by Mr Reed, the late Chief Constructor of the Navy, and embodied by him in a paper read before the Institution of Naval Architects in the spring of 1868."

The calculations Barnaby referred to showed that when the edge of the deck of a low-sided ship was awash and she continued to heel over, the maximum stability – or righting force of the vessel – was soon reached, and thereafter it diminished rapidly until the ship lost all power to recover herself. But this remained little more than an interesting theory until the loss of the *Captain* brought out its full significance.

As Barnaby pointed out: "Despite the danger I then foresaw, I should not have presumed to press these calculations in the face of the officers who tried the *Captain.* It would be a presumption to do so, because it was impossible to submit to calculation the height of the waves, the force of the wind and other circumstances. After the ship was lost these calculations have been held to show *why* she was lost, and they do partly explain it. But so far as I am aware, no one predicted from these calculations that the *Captain* would turn over. Had I thought so I should have felt it my duty, notwithstanding the awkwardness of the position as between ourselves, Captain Coles, and the designers of the ship, to have said so.

"I should have been prepared to have been told that the calculations were fallacious. I may say, as a matter of fact, that the precisely similar calculations made by me for the two-decked ships cut down, and already referred to, were sent by their Lordships to a distinguished naval architect, Mr Isaac Watts, formerly Chief Constructor of the Navy (he having endorsed the proposals to cut down such ships), and he discredited the calculation, stating that it was a question of strength of masts versus stiffness (resistance to tilting) of the ship."

Captain Rice took up the questioning: "In point of fact, the idea entertained was that the *Captain* would be so steady a ship that there was comparatively little danger of her ever lurching or rolling to the angle of 54 degrees at which I understand her stability vanished?"

"That is exactly so."

"It has been stated that the ship was about two feet deeper in the water than she should have been: was that so?"

"The ship was two feet deeper in the water than the design prepared by Messrs Laird and Captain Coles provided for," replied Barnaby, making it clear that he was not going to be understood to say at what depth *he* thought the ship should have floated – which was one way of interpreting the question.

"Did Lairds furnish with their design, before the ship was built, any detailed statement of all the weights going to make up the sum of the weight of hull and equipment?"

"They furnished the particulars shown in the documents supplied to the court. It will be seen that the weight of the hull is stated to be 3000 tons: no details were given as to how this 3000 tons was to be made up. There was a specification, but it was necessarily too incomplete to enable this to be accurately checked. It would have taken some three or four weeks to do it, had we had the information, and when it was done we should have had no control over the manner in which Lairds built the

125

ship from the specification, so that they might have departed from it even had it been verified.

"My own evidence in these printed particulars shows that when I first saw the ship in her very early stage, I saw that there was no evidence of the care and vigilance which are found to be necessary in armoured ships in order to secure the precise draught of water. Lairds, I believe, weighed very carefully the materials which they put into the ship, but I saw in the distribution of the materials many instances of too large an amount of material expended in order to produce the desired results in strength of structure."

The President asked Barnaby if he could give any example of the degree of accuracy with which ships constructed in the Royal Dockyards floated, as compared with the level at which they were designed to float.

"I can," replied Barnaby. "I may say that the *Monarch* came precisely to her designed line, but I must say further, in justice to Messrs Laird, that I have known cases of wide departure from the designed draught of water.

"It must be borne in mind that an error of five per cent in the thickness of plates and angle irons with which the ship is built – an error of which the manufacturers of the iron would think nothing – would, if it were all an error on the thick side, as it usually would be, cause a ship of war as ordinarily constructed to sink five inches deeper in the water than designed for."

The President: "I can see that in Mr Reed's report on the design of the *Captain*, when it was being considered by the Admiralty, he says that the reduction in the height of the armoured side of the ship, as compared with the *Monarch*, enables the designer to obtain the requisite stability with a reduced beam. Is there any sort of rule as to the amount of requisite stability for ships constructed at the Admiralty? That is, what is the least point of inclination at which the maximum point of stability should be found, and to what amount of heel should the ship be capable of falling over with safety, and with the power of recovering herself?"

Barnaby: "In ordinary ships the stability, or righting power, is least when the ship is upright, and it goes on increasing in amount so long as there is any height of side to immerse, the increase being nearly in proportion to the increase in the angle. But the words used by Mr Reed, 'the requisite stability', do not apply, I imagine, to this angle, but to the distance between the centre of gravity and the metacentre (the righting pendulum).

"There is no absolute rule for this, but we have found that in iron-cased ships of large size, where this distance is about three feet the ship has the requisite stability and steadiness. Mr Reed distinctly guarded himself against being supposed to have calculated the stability of the ship in the three days during which the drawings were in his hands. Such calculations, if he had possessed the information required – which he did not – would have taken him as many weeks."

At this point Captain Commerell, V.C., sought to place some responsibility upon E. J. Reed for not having warned the officers of the *Captain* of the facts about the ship's stability. Reed was to give evidence before the court himself later but, in the meantime, Barnaby took care of his reputation.

Captain Commerell said: "Holding the views Mr Reed did relative to the masting of low freeboard vessels, do you consider that before sanctioning the sail plan, which he thought large, it would have been as well to have at least warned the Flag Officers and Captain Burgoyne what a tender ship they had to deal with, so that she might have had exceptional treatment?"

"I have already stated that Mr Reed had only about three days in which to consider this design before making his report of July 20th 1866," replied Barnaby. "When that was forwarded their Lordships were informed that a more careful examination of the drawings and specifications would be necessary if any responsibility were to be placed upon him. On July 23rd, no further investigation having been made, their Lordships approved of the ship on the responsibility of Captain Coles and Messrs Lairds; and Mr Reed was so informed."

"Am I to understand that in the peculiar circumstances under which the *Captain* was built, the Chief Constructor considered that the whole of the responsibility of the ship and the 500 men it contained was removed from his office?"

There was a slightly aggressive edge to Captain Commerell's voice as he, a practical sailor, put this question to one of the men responsible for designing the ships he and his kind had to sail. He probably had no conception of what was involved in calculations that would take three weeks to work out.

"I can best answer that," said Barnaby, "by quoting from the Controller's summary of events leading up to the building of the *Captain*, where he remarks: 'Their Lordships are quite aware that neither the design nor the specification met with my entire approval, and accepted both with that knowledge. The responsibility of the design must rest with Captain Coles and Messrs Laird, and nothing but the duty of seeing the designs rigidly adhered to and worked out faithfully, both as regards materials and labour, has been entrusted to the Controller's department.'"

"I am, then," Commerell insisted, "to understand that the moment that letter was written, expressing the Chief Constructor's view as to his opinion of the designs of the *Captain* not having met with his entire approval, any responsibility – not for the success of the experiment but for the actual safety of the ship – was removed?"

"The Controller of the Navy never supposed, I understand from the correspondence I have seen, and from what I know of the facts, that the *Captain* would be in danger of capsizing. His objections to her on the ground of want of seaworthiness were, as I understand it, never pushed on this point. It is inconceivable that, having any such fear, he should have declined the responsibility."

Captain Rice: "Is there any question among naval architects as to the theoretical truth concerning the relative safety of high and low freeboard ships?"

"Undoubtedly there is," said Barnaby. "Mr Henwood, a member of the Institution of Naval Architects, has advocated persistently for years that line-of-battle ships be cut down to three or four feet freeboard and heavily masted. And what he has said has been endorsed by large numbers of persons assuming to be authorities."

"So that," said Rice, "Naval officers and unscientific men may doubt to which side of the scientific view they should bow?"

It may be supposed that Barnaby smiled faintly: "They may," he said.

Among the mass of technical evidence with which the court was supplied there had been reference made to foot-tons when describing the righting force of various ships. Captain Commerell now asked for an explanation of the term from Barnaby, as an expert in such matters.

"The righting force of a ship," he replied, "may be considered to be the weight of a ship at the end of the arm of a lever. If the length of the arm were two feet and the weight of the ship is 1000 tons, then the number of foot-tons in her righting force would be 2×1000; so that if the weight of the ship were doubled, i.e. 2000 tons, she would have the same righting force if the lever were only one foot long."

In Commerell's next and last question came the crux of the whole matter, the foundation for that part of the court's findings which were to have such repercussions.

"I am under the impression, drawn from the usual sources of information in part, and partly from the summary which has been laid before the court, that the construction of this ship was forced upon the Board of Admiralty by what is termed public opinion, in the periodical papers of the day, and in the Houses of Parliament. Now, what is your opinion on that point, who, from the beginning to end must have been cognizant of everything connected with this affair?"

The Judge Advocate intervened and advised Barnaby that there was no need for him to answer this question if he did not think it proper to do so.

Barnaby, however, was not afraid to say what he thought – in his wordy Whitehall way.

"This view," he said, "is that which was always entertained in the Department of the Controller of the Navy."

Less diplomatically, he could have said that an ignorant clamour had led the Admiralty into doing something it had been advised by its experts not to do.

CHAPTER 17

SHARING THE BLAME

Among the hundreds who grieved over the loss of dear ones in the *Captain* disaster, and those who may have had misgivings about the part they had played in persuading the Admiralty to have her built, there were two men to whom the loss of the ship was also a loss of reputation – William and Henry Laird, the brothers who carried on at Birkenhead, on the river Mersey, the family business of building ships. William Laird now came before the court to tell his story.

He said they had not previously built such a big ship of design similar to the *Captain*, or one with the special arrangement of the hurricane deck above the main deck for working the sails.

They had made approximate calculations of the ship's centre of gravity in 1866 from the design, and a more complete calculation was made after the ship was completed in January 1870.

"In the case of the calculations made in 1866 we felt that in a ship of a novel type, with a distribution of weights differing in many respects from other ships, it was difficult in the then state of the design to arrive at as accurate a result as we could have done if the ship had been of a more ordinary type, or the construction of the ship further advanced."

Various other calculations of its stability were made with the ship presumed to be at various angles, but nothing was seen in these figures to cause alarm. In fact, the firm seemed to have followed the usual practice of the time in building the ship. Any method of doing almost anything can appear to be lax or inefficient when subjected to the probing and cross-examination of a court. It was never suggested that Lairds were responsible, by their methods, for the inherent fault in the ship, although there was a good deal of questioning about their procedures at Birkenhead.

"Did you make any calculations to determine how the stability of the ship would be affected by the gunwale being under water?" asked the President.

"We made no calculations, but discussed the matter and were of opinion that the stability would go on increasing for some time after the gunwale was immersed, and although not calculated, it agreed nearly with the statement of the calculations made after the inclining of the ship by the Admiralty."

"What did you consider to be the limiting angle of safe sailing in the *Captain*, and did you express your opinion on this point to any person in authority on board the ship?"

"In conversation as to pressing the *Captain* under sail I have alluded to the gunwale as being the limit, but without mentioning the particular angle as it varied slightly with the draught of water of the ship (according to weights and stores aboard). But the impression on my mind, and I think generally, was that it would be seldom necessary to press the ship so far, although we all felt sure there was a considerable reserve beyond this."

"Did that conversation take place with Captain Burgoyne?"

"We had more than once spoken on the subject, but only as conversation."

"Had you any conversation on the subject with Captain Coles?"

"I remember, on the occasion of one of the trial trips under steam, having a somewhat similar conversation with Captain Coles."

"Why did you not ascertain by experiment the position of the centre of gravity of the *Captain* before she left Birkenhead?"

"It is an experiment we are not in the habit of making, and the difficulties of making it at Birkenhead, and the chances of error after it had been made, would have been much greater than at Portsmouth, because when the ship left Birkenhead she had on board none of her stores, nor her guns, nor her boats, sails, or the whole of her running rigging, and it was in view of these considerations that on February 21st we wrote to Captain Coles."

This letter and those deriving from it are given in some detail because they show how fate arranged for the vital experiment to be delayed until it was virtually too late to save the ship. It was not from any lurking doubts about the stability of the *Captain*, but, rather, from scientific interest that Lairds wrote to Coles on this matter. Coles's reply showed how anxious he was to get the ship to sea and enjoy the moment he had been working and waiting for for a decade; the day when a ship designed expressly to carry his turntable turrets should sail and prove herself to be the equal and master of any ship in the British Navy – or any other navy.

From Lairds to Captain Coles: 21 February 1870:

"Experiments were made to ascertain by inclining them with weights in the steam basin, the centre of weight and stability of several classes of ironclad broadside ships. . . . We think that it would be desirable to have similar experiments tried on the *Captain*. The reasons given for trying the experiments alluded to were stated to be that as they (the iron-clads) differed from the old types of wooden ships it was desirable to ascertain how far this difference affected their stability, and the same reasons hold good for the *Captain*, which differs in her disposition of weights from the ships already experimented on.

"We enclose a letter which we think would bring the matter in a proper way before the Admiralty and shall be glad to know what you think of it, and to receive back the letter with any comments you wish to make."

Coles replied to Lairds on 22 February 1870, from:

> Mountfield,
> Bonchurch,
> Isle of Wight.

> "With reference to your letter of February 21st containing proposal to try experiments on the stability of the *Captain* by means of moving weights in her in the steam basin. It is purely a naval architects' and shipbuilders' question, and therefore is a matter in which I would not wish to interfere: subject to this observation however, I would remark that any experiments that in any way would delay her going for her sea-going trial, or are not actually necessary, would be better postponed until after her coming cruise."

On 24 February Lairds wrote to the Controller of the Navy. For them it was a fortuitous letter, because it placed on record their request, at an early date, for the vital experiment to be carried out: although they had no idea what its real significance would be, or that delaying it would lead to the possibility of disaster. Nevertheless, in the circumstances, it was a useful letter to have written.

"To the Controller of the Navy. February 24th 1870

"Referring to your letter of August 9th, 1866, on the question of the disposition of weights in relation to the centre of displacement and consequent stability of the *Captain*. We beg to submit that now she is complete and *before she proceeds to sea*, a careful experiment should be made by inclining by weights in the steam basin to ascertain the position . . . of the centre of gravity with greater certainty than is possible by calculation.

"The importance of such experiments has been acknowledged . . . It was felt that iron-cased ships differed so much from all preceding ships in many respects that it was highly necessary some such experiment should be made; and as these ships differed from ships not armour-clad, so the *Captain* may be said to differ in many respects from other ironclad ships,

132

and hence our reason for requesting that their Lordships will allow similar experiments to be made with the *Captain*."

On the recommendation of E. J. Reed, the Controller of the Navy, Sir Spencer Robinson, replied to Lairds on 26 February 1870:

"I am commanded by my Lords, the Commissioners of the Admiralty, to acquaint you in reply to your letter of the 24th that steps shall be taken to ascertain the vertical height of the *Captain*'s centre of gravity when an opportunity offers, and the weather is settled; but that it is not considered desirable to attempt to carry out the experiment before the forthcoming trials are completed, or while the weather is so unsettled."

No doubt the weather was unsuitable, but the very fact of Reed's having recommended such a reply shows that he had no serious concern for the actual safety of the *Captain* at that time – despite what he was to say to the court later.

The President quoted to Laird a passage from an Admiralty letter to Captain Coles: "'Their Lordships approve of a ship being built on this design as proposed, on the entire responsibility of Captain Coles and Messrs Laird.' *Was* the ship designed upon the entire responsibility of your firm and Captain Coles?" he asked.

This was not a suggestion that Laird could accept without damaging his firm's reputation as ship designers and builders.

"We did not consider so," he replied, "and the letter from the Secretary of the Admiralty, dated April 24th, 1866, requesting our co-operation in carrying into effect their Lordships's wishes, will show why we considered ourselves not entirely responsible."

This was the letter that must have given so much pleasure to Coles; the letter that meant, after years of perseverance, he was at last going to be allowed to put his guns into a ship of his own conception.

"Their Lordships, in this letter," said Laird, "reserved the right of approving the design submitted and also the tender that might be submitted. And if it was found inexpedient to enter into such a contract, they would be free to decline to build the ship, but in that case would defray the cost of preparing the designs."

This was true: but in a further letter to Lairds some very important paragraphs appear, which were almost prophetic in their implication, as it turned out. The Admiralty wrote:

"It is proper you should be made aware that your design, in its structural details, is not in all respects satisfactory to their Lordships . . . the hull appears somewhat heavily designed in places and the weight allowed for this, barely sufficient. No allowance appears to be made for the weight of the engines for working the capstans and turrets. It is very desirable that you should thoroughly satisfy yourselves in regard to the weight and the position of the centre of gravity which, in a ship so armoured and plated, will probably be found to be high . . ."

In reply to this Laird wrote: "The design proposed by us in conjunction with Captain Coles, has our entire approval . . . and we are quite willing to accept, with Captain Coles, the joint responsibility of having recommended their Lordships to build a vessel on the plans submitted. . . . We do not object to the works being carried on under the inspection of an Admiralty officer, on the terms stated, such inspection not to relieve us from the responsibility of the details of construction. . . . We have carefully considered the position of the centre of gravity and the disposition of the weights, and have no reason to fear that the vessel will be deficient in the stability necessary."

Laird went on to explain how every plan of every detail of the ship was made in triplicate. One copy was sent to the Controller and work was not proceeded with until this copy was received back approved or 'not objected to'. A copy was sent to Captain Coles whose health prevented his being in Birkenhead for the building of the ship; and a third copy was kept by Lairds as a record. In this way the three parties with any responsibility for the construction were kept informed of every step.

The resident Admiralty inspector on the job had been kept informed of the weight of iron put into the ship; but when the *Captain* floated for the first time Laird said it was obvious that she was heavier than planned and settled deeper in the water than intended. Both Captain Coles and the Controller of the Navy, Sir Spencer Robinson, were officially informed of this.

President: "So in point of fact your view of the case may be briefly stated thus: that after the conclusion of the contract with the Admiralty, your responsibility for the designs of the *Captain* became precisely what it would have been for any other ship, the designs and specifications of which had been sent to you from the Admiralty?"

Laird: "We considered that it took away from us the sole responsibility of the design: but we had stated on August 15th that 'the design prepared by us in conjunction with Captain Coles has our entire approval', and again, 'We are quite willing to accept with Captain Coles the joint responsibility of having recommended their Lordships to build the vessel on the plan submitted', but we should not have ventured on the sole responsibility."

President: "Therefore, then, I understand that you consider the responsibility between yourselves and Captain Coles on the one hand, and the Admiralty on the other, was a joint responsibility?"

"Inasmuch as the plans and specifications had been submitted to the Admiralty in the terms of their letter of April 24th, 1866, we consider that they had their approval, or that they would not have invited us to submit a tender for the ship."

Considering in retrospect the position of Lairds, and the admissions and confident assertions they had made in writing to the Admiralty at a time when there was a likelihood of their obtaining a £335,000 contract, William Laird's anxiety to relieve his firm of sole responsibility is understandable.

But, it may be wondered, how much credit for the design, and responsibility for its construction, would have been freely offered to the Admiralty had things turned out differently and, instead of having the angle of doom built into her, HMS *Captain* had proved herself the match or superior of every ship in the fleet, both in sailing and gunnery, and had completely vindicated Coles's years of campaigning for his invention. It is more than likely that their Lordships – and E. J. Reed in particular – would have been the objects of triumphant obloquy from all those, qualified and unqualified, who had supported Coles in his feud with the Chief Constructor.

"Supposing," Admiral Yelverton asked, "you had known the results of the calculations made, and that the stability of the *Captain* vanished entirely at an inclination of 54 degrees, would you, as her designers, have felt at all uneasy as to her safety as a sea-going ship?"

"No," replied Laird.

"Did you mast the *Captain* with reference to her tonnage, as though she had been a high freeboard ship, and not consider the low freeboard might make it necessary she should carry less canvas?"

"We did not consider that the low freeboard would make it necessary to have spars smaller than were fitted. In the preparation of the plan for the spars, Captain Coles, from his knowledge of the subject, necessarily took a prominent part, but we did not see it necessary to remonstrate with him in any way; nor did we feel any apprehension in our own minds."

Frank though this reply appears to be, it nevertheless shifted responsibility for the *Captain*'s top heavy rigging with low freeboard to Coles, with the implication that he was an expert in naval architecture, which he was not in a technical and theoretical sense: few sailors were in those days. The impression was given that although Lairds were not shirking their share of responsibility, their fault was more one of failing to see the danger through inexpertness in this specialised branch of ship design.

There was little more that Laird could say to assist the court – or his firm.

CHAPTER 18

THE VERDICT OF SAILORS

It was almost as if some instinctive sense of the dramatic had made the court save its most interesting witness until last; for now came E. J. Reed, former Chief Constructor of the Navy, the 56th witness and the man who had been proved tragically right in his opposition to Captain Coles. That, most certainly, is how Reed would have seen the decade of dissent between Coles and himself.

After a few formal questions to establish his identity and position in the public service, the President said to Reed:

"From various statements which appear in the Admiralty summary of correspondence leading up to the construction of the *Captain*, and the evidence of Messrs Barnaby and Barnes, who were Assistant Constructors when you held the office of Chief Constructor, and from this sentence in an Admiralty letter – 'Their Lordships approve of a ship being built on this design as proposed *on the entire responsibility of Captain Coles and Messrs Laird*' – from this I was led to the belief that Messrs Laird and Captain Coles were solely responsible for the design of the ship.

"But from further evidence which has been given before us by Messrs Laird, it would appear that they were and still are under the conviction that the responsibility as between the Controller of the Navy, and the departments under his direction, was jointly with them, and they have adduced in support of this conviction the circumstances that at various times communications were forwarded to the Admiralty relative to details of construction, and were returned to them approved, or not objected to. Will you be good enough to state to the court your opinion on this matter?"

The heavy, severe face of E. J. Reed, man of science, object of criticism both in and out of Parliament and in the Press for his opposition to the revolutionary views of Captain Coles on ship design, showed little, if any, sign that this was his moment of triumph in the controversy, of vindication of his unpopular opinions.

He was a good speaker and, for a civil servant, had been most vocal in defending Admiralty policy and his own designs. Although he could not but have been aware of the sense of tragedy that hung over these proceedings, they were, none the less, his opportunity.

"I am of opinion that the responsibility for this design must rest entirely upon Captain Coles and Messrs Laird," he said. "Because the court will observe that in the last reports made upon the design by the Controller of the Navy and myself prior to the commencement of the ship, we both cast doubts upon the character of the design. I, in particular, questioned it upon two points with reference to which it has failed – its floatation and stability.

"It is out of the question to suppose that their Lordships would order £335,000 of the public money to be expended upon, and 500 lives committed to, a ship the responsibility for which was to rest upon persons who had from the beginning believed the characteristic feature of the ship to be wrong, and out of whose hands the design of the ship and the responsibility for it had been advisedly and distinctly taken in order to put to the test the question whether our belief that a high freeboard was necessary in a fully rigged sailing vessel was a mere prejudice of ours – or a scientific conviction."

Reed had a firm grip on his audience and there was no doubt a tenseness in the court as the long lucid sentences rolled out.

"The very cause of the *Captain*'s being designed and of her being built was the assumption that the opinions of Sir Spencer Robinson and myself were not to be trusted, and that we were showing some prejudiced opposition to the views of Captain Coles.

"So strongly did I feel that we were clear of responsibility for this ship, and that the time would come when it would be necessary for us to prove our exemption from that responsibility, that I forbade my assistants ever to employ the phrase 'approved' even for the most minor details, and I directed them never to employ a stronger phrase (even with regard to the smallest details) than 'no objection would be offered'.

"If the word 'approved', applied even to the minutest detail of the *Captain*, ever left my office, it was from an oversight resulting in a disregard of that general instruction. If, therefore, Captain Coles and Messrs Laird were not responsible for the success and seaworthiness of the *Captain*, no naval officer and no naval architect was responsible for it."

No clearer rejection of responsibility could have been made. Reed had even foreseen this very argument and taken precautions accordingly.

Vice-Admiral Yelverton asked:

"Had you at any time from the first commencement of the *Captain*'s construction up to the time of her loss, any misgivings as to her stability and seaworthiness?"

"Undoubtedly."

137

"Did it occur to you that the calculations as to her displacement were wanting in accuracy?"

"As regards the weights to be carried, the inaccuracy of the calculation became evident after the ship was floated: but before she was commenced, I twice over referred in my reports to the risk of excess weight being incurred from what the design alone showed, and I specified some weights which had not apparently been considered."

Reed was referring here to his report on the original drawings in which he said no allowance, among other things, had been made for the weight of the engines needed to drive the capstans and the turrets.

"You say you had some misgivings as to her seaworthiness and stability: will you say in what way?"

"The misgiving I had as to her seaworthiness is obvious from the fact that I advocated a high freeboard in order to secure seaworthiness. The grounds upon which I believed her unseaworthy since her completion are first that I believed her funnel casings, which would be subject to such forcings as no other ship that I know of is liable to, were likely to be started and even carried away in extremely heavy weather, and the consequences would be that the large engine and boiler hatches would be at once open to the inroads of the sea, and the ship would be likely to founder.

"In the next place, I believe that with little or no sail set the *Captain*, as completed, was liable on encountering waves to be made to roll heavily and I am not at all sure that when so rolling, should she ship a heavy sea on the windward side, her topweights would not be at once so greatly augmented as to carry her past her position of maximum stability, and capsize her – this liability resulting from the absence of anything like a sufficient escape for the sea across the deck and beneath the hurricane deck.

"And thirdly, I cannot doubt that the *Captain* was deficient of that growing stability, which a ship with a high side possesses, to such a degree as to bring about the accident which appears to have happened.

"All these grounds of apprehension applied to her service in time of peace. As regards her capability in action, I do not like to express to this court the sense I feel of the unfitness of a 4000-ton ship with a deck six and a half feet high, with engine and boiler hatches protected only by thin iron casing, to fight an action with a risk of encountering a breeze of wind afterwards."

"Were you kept acquainted with all the alterations suggested by Captain Coles and carried out by Messrs Laird during her construction?"

"Yes, when the alterations were directed to specified parts of her design laid down by the Admiralty. Not with reference to other aspects of design."

"On visiting the *Captain* did it strike you at any time that she was heavily masted in every way, and that the corresponding spread of canvas would far exceed what is usual in a ship of her size?"

"I should have considered the ordinary masting excessive for a ship like the *Captain*," said Reed, "and I have never yet been able to ascertain on what grounds anyone pretended or could pretend that the *Captain* with her spread of canvas, and her actual height of deck, was fit to carry the same sail as other ships of her size, and to encounter gusts and squalls to which every squadron sailing ship is liable."

"From your scientific and practical knowledge and talent as a great shipbuilder, can you account in any way for the cause or partial cause of the *Captain*'s foundering as she did?"

Reed had no hesitation in answering this. He did not actually say 'I told you so', of course, but it was difficult to hide the satisfaction in his reply.

"As soon as the news of the *Captain*'s disappearance came to this country I concluded that she had capsized under the pressure of her canvas; and while I believe, from such information as one can gather, that it might have been quite practical so to reduce the canvas on the night of her loss as to save her, my conviction is that the evil day would only have been deferred and that there was nothing in the management of the *Captain* on the night of her loss which would have occasioned the loss of any other ship in the squadron."

In other words, Reed was saying that there was nothing wrong with Captain Burgoyne's seamanship – only with his ship.

Captain Hancock: "Do you imagine, from what you know of the loss of the *Captain*, that it was in any way attributable to either of the two elements of danger you have alluded to; namely, the sea bursting into the funnel casing from to leeward, or that a heavy sea shipped to windward added so largely to her topweight as to destroy her stability."

Reed: "I have seen no evidence tending to show that the funnel casings were broken through, but I think it much more likely that she shipped a considerable weight of sea to windward than that the pressure of wind acting upon the underside of the hurricane deck seriously contributed to her loss."

"I gather from the views you have expressed of the construction of the *Captain* that no reduction of masts would have made her a seaworthy ship," said Captain Rice. "Is that so?"

"It is."

"Have you any reason to suppose that Captain Burgoyne was aware of your views of the unseaworthiness of his ship?"

Again Reed was ready with the complete answer to the suggestion that he might not have made his views known to those whom they most vitally concerned.

"Yes. I spoke to Captain Burgoyne in the same sense in which I have answered the court, as far as opportunity offered, and when I left the ship at Birkenhead the last time I saw Captain Burgoyne, I said to him, 'I don't want to say any more against her; but I am glad that it is your fate and not mine to go to sea in her.'

"I also knew that a friend of mine, an admiral in the service, took great pains to impress upon Captain Burgoyne that particular danger of her capsizing under her canvas to which reference has been made. And in mentioning his conversation in writing to me on the day that the loss was reported, but before the mode of the loss was known, he referred to my remarks on rigging ships with low freeboard. He said he had drawn the serious attention of Captain Burgoyne to the position of the ship's deck, but that the confidence of Captain Burgoyne was such that it almost defied criticism."

"Do you consider that the Lords Commissioners of the Admiralty who ordered the construction of the *Captain* removed, as far as the design of the *Captain* went, the Controllership from Sir Spencer Robinson to Captain Coles, and the Chief Constructorship from yourself to Messrs Laird; and that, in point of fact, this responsibility rests upon the Board who ordered her construction, notwithstanding the known objection of the Controller and Chief Constructor?"

Reed could hardly have put the matter more to his own satisfaction himself.

"Yes," he replied. "And notwithstanding their own objections also: for the Sea Lords of the Admiralty without exception that I can remember, have been unfavourable to the rigging of ships with low freeboard, although it was out of my power to say whether this unfavourableness arose to any extent from their apprehension of danger."

"Do you know when the decision to build the *Captain* irrespective of approving specification, etc, was taken?"

"I cannot speak with certainty, but I believe that from the time that Captain Coles condemned the *Monarch* as in no degree representing his views, their Lordships were strongly disposed, if not actually determined, to yield to the strongly expressed opinion of some Members of Parliament, and to build a ship from Captain Coles's designs."

"In fact, the *Captain* was built in compliance with strong outside pressure on the Admiralty?"

"I have no doubt of that," said Reed.

Captain Commerell was still more concerned with how much Captain Burgoyne knew about the stability of his ship.

"Do you think," he asked, "that with a diagram like the one the court has seen, together with a full intimation that 21 degrees was the point which would assuredly capsize the *Captain*, and that in dealing with the *Captain* the same as other ships entailed a grave responsibility, this would have had a great influence upon the officers entrusted with the experiment? I ask this as an officer who has had the *Captain* under his orders and who, with that diagram before him, would not have dared to keep the ship under sail one single night?"

"The *Captain* was built expressly to be under the same conditions as other ships," replied Reed. "And I believe, although I regret to have to state it, that if any such intimation had emanated from the Admiralty it would have resulted in the strongest possible efforts to prove the Admiralty wrong, and to carry all sail possible.

"But however this may be, it clearly was a part of the responsibility that Captain Coles and Messrs Laird undertook, to give to the captain of the ship, who was present with the ship for many months before she left the dock, whatever information they considered necessary to preserve the lives of those on board from those dangers which I had great personal trouble to ascertain and to point out, only to have them repudiated by those who did most to encourage a belief in the safety of rigged sailing ships with low freeboard. But so far were the responsible designers of the ship from giving any such warning that they were to some extent parties to these trials, and to those reports which filled others with confidence, and myself and a limited few with consternation."

But this was not good enough for Captain Commerell, who appeared to be unwilling to accept the pre-vision and expertise of Mr Reed.

"Were you not aware that Messrs Laird fully believed in the stability and seaworthiness of their ship?" he asked. "And you, on the other hand, were as certainly aware of her utter unseaworthiness. Do you not think that it would have been better if you had requested that official information should be given to Captain Burgoyne of the danger you saw him plunging into, and not left it to Captain Coles, who you knew, as an inventor, was perfectly blind to anything but the merits of his own invention, to give information which you knew would be fatal?"

This was a question that, if not rejected firmly, threw responsibility for the disaster to some extent upon Reed. He left no room for doubt in his reply.

"I do not think it would have been better for me to have done anything which I did not do. My belief was and is that the unseaworthiness of

141

the *Captain* was a cause of anxiety to many who professed to believe in her, and what I thought would happen with the *Captain* was this: that she would have the highest possible reports to begin with, that she would be very carefully nursed through her early career until her deficiencies became slowly admitted, and that before she got through a commission she would be condemned as utterly unfit for the naval service.

"I should state to the court that, in order to prevent several years of protestation against this ship, resulting at last in some possible compromise of myself, nearly a year ago I did what I thought was right in the matter in resisting to the utmost degree in my power a desire on the part of the First Lord of the Admiralty to increase the number of *Captains*, and to place persons possessing no knowledge of scientific principles in a position to influence the designs of Her Majesty's ships.

"That resistance I repeated, and again repeated, and again repeated, and in each of my repetitions based my position upon the danger which was involved in the *Captain* herself, and when I found that my resistance was useless I retired from duty, and undertook to submit the resignation of my office. The proposals in question were withdrawn, but the court will draw its own inferences from the two facts – that I am out of office and the son of the First Lord is among the unhappy victims of this loss.

"I wish the court to believe that my actual departure from office at length did not arise from this cause, but this cause had its weight in all that has happened, and the court will perhaps see that I had the strongest reasons for not keeping up a systematic assertion of the danger incurred in the *Captain.*"

At the time of Reed's resignation in the previous July there had been no public knowledge of the heated antagonism between Reed, the civil servant, and Childers, First Lord and political head of the Admiralty. But Childers had become completely convinced of the soundness of Coles's ideas, and the more Reed opposed him the more their relationship deteriorated.

At the time of the earlier successful trials of the *Captain*, when Coles's credit at the Admiralty soared (at least as far as the First Lord was concerned), there was an intimation given him that some more profitable use might be made of his services at the Admiralty. Coles referred to the fact several times in his various reports on the trials and there is little doubt that this is what Reed was referring to when he spoke of "persons possessing no knowledge of scientific principles" being introduced in the construction department. The idea of having Coles in his department was, of course, insufferable.

The President had one more question: "Mr Reed, these diagrams we have seen: the angles of stability shown are, of course, merely graphic representations of the results of calculations and of no virtue in themselves, would you say?"

Reed had one more rather ironic answer: "Just so: except the virtue of showing the extreme danger of an ironclad turret ship which had so low a side as to bring her deck into the water at a moderate angle of inclination."

*   *   *

That concluded what might be described as the evidence for the 'prosecution', since this was a court martial of May and the other survivors. It was now May's turn to submit his defence. In fact, of course, there was no need for him to defend himself, since the evidence had disclosed nothing to his discredit. He therefore made a simple statement to the court, in the language of his time, of what he thought were relevant matters.

"After all that has been adduced in evidence it is unnecessary for me to take up your time by further details respecting the loss of HMS *Captain*," he said. "I therefore beg to state that I have been 23 years in Her Majesty's Navy, 11 years of which as a warrant officer. But I am unable to produce testimonials for that period of service, as I have inadvertently lost them.

"I therefore place myself in the hands of this most honourable court, trusting that they will exonerate me, as well as the other survivors, from all blame . . .

"I also wish to bring to your notice the excellent conduct of the survivors when in my charge, both in the launch and ashore; more especially that of Charles Tregenna, leading seaman, who for about 10 hours so ably managed the steer oar, and on whose courage to a certain extent our safety depended: also that of James Ellis, Gunner's Mate, who, as senior petty officer, assisted me in every way . . .

"In conclusion, on behalf of the survivors and myself I beg to tender our most sincere thanks for the great kindness shown towards us during this present trial by the President and members of the most honourable court."

In this way the proceedings came to an end for the time being: it was 4 October. The court sat again on 11 October, when the President read out the findings.

"The court," he said, "having heard the statement of Mr James May and taken his evidence and that of the remaining survivors and other evidence they deemed necessary, and having deliberately weighed and considered the whole of the evidence before them, do find that Her Majesty's ship *Captain* was capsized on the morning of the 7th September 1870 by pressure of sail, assisted by the heave of the sea, and that the sail

143

carried at the time of her loss (regard being had to the force of the wind and state of the sea) was insufficient to have endangered a ship endued with the proper amount of stability.

"The court further find that no blame is attributable to Mr James May, Gunner 2nd Class, and the surviving Petty Officers and men of Her Majesty's ship *Captain*, for her loss, and do therefore fully acquit them of all blame in respect of it."

This was no more than had been expected throughout the country. But the court did not leave it at that. They went on to announce one of the most serious condemnations of Government and certain people that has ever been made by an officially constituted court.

"The court, before separating, find it their duty to record the conviction they entertain that the *Captain* was built in deference to public opinion expressed in Parliament, and through other channels, and in opposition to the views and opinions of the Controller and his department, and that the evidence all tends to show that they generally disapproved of her construction.

"It further appearing in evidence that before the *Captain* was received from the contractors a gross departure from her original design had been committed, whereby her draught of water was increased about two feet and her freeboard was diminished to a corresponding extent, and that her stability proved to be dangerously small, combined with an area of sail, under those circumstances, excessive. The court deeply regret that if these facts were duly known and appreciated, they were not communicated to the officer in command of the ship, or that, if otherwise, the ship was allowed to be employed in the ordinary service of the Fleet before they had been ascertained by calculation and experience."

The ripple of excitement that ran through the courtroom died away as the President rose and called upon May to stand forward at the table of the court.

As May came to attention before him the President picked up the Gunner's sword, which lay on the table, hilt towards May, and handed it back to him in the traditional gesture of acquittal.

"Mr May," he said, "I am desired by the court, to avail myself of the present occasion to acquaint you and the other survivors of the crew of the *Captain*, that the court is satisfied you made every effort consistent with your duty to save more of your shipmates; and further, that the court is of opinion that their conduct, together with your own, during the period they were under your command, reflects credit on yourself and on the service to which you belong."

"Thank you, sir," said May. And the enquiry, officially, was over for the time being.

HMS *Captain* alongside in a Royal Dockyard. *(Courtesy of Imperial War Museum, London. Neg. No. Q21074)*

Survivors from HMS *Captain, Front row:* James Saunders, John Heard, Charles Tregenna, John Walker, James Freeman, John Gribble. *Centre row:* Francis Merryman, Robert Tomlinson, James Ellis, James May, William Lawrence, Henry Grange, David Dryburgh. *Rear row:* James Harvey, Robert Herd, Thomas Kernan, Lewis Werry, George Bride. Identified from named individual photographs in the National Maritime Museum. *(Courtesy of National Maritime Museum, Greenwich. Neg. No. A2545)*

Artist's impression of HMS *Captain* as she was shortly before she foundered.
(Courtesy of National Maritime Museum, Greenwich. Neg. No. 58/3257)

HMS *Devastation*, completed in 1873, was the first ocean-going mastless man-of-war and may be regarded as the forerunner of battleships as they have been known in the 20th century.
(Courtesy of Imperial War Museum, London. Neg. No. Q38631)

HMS *Dreadnought*, last of the ironclads, was in service for 25 years from 1879 and was loved throughout the Royal Navy. *(Courtesy of Imperial War Museum, London. Neg. No. Q21186A)*

HMS *Trafalgar*, the last single citadel turret ship to be built in Britain, and the first to mount a secondary armament of quick-firing 6-in. guns in addition to the two 13.5-in. guns in each turret. *(Courtesy of Imperial War Museum, London. Neg. No. Q40357)*

HMS *Royal Sovereign*, designed by Sir William White, gave her name to a class of capital ships, combining efficiency with handsome appearance. *(Courtesy of Imperial War Museum, London. Neg. No. Q40047)*

HMS *Majestic*, designed by Sir William White, represented the peak of Victorian battleship design, both in efficiency and elegance. *(Courtesy of Imperial War Museum, London. Neg. No. Q39494)*

CHAPTER 19

WHY DIDN'T THEY ASK KERNAN?

A curious fact about the court martial of the survivors is that no member of the court asked how the launch came to float clear of the sinking ship as the sea advanced inexorably up the steepening deck while the *Captain* was rolling to her final resting place on the sea bed.

Several survivors were asked how they managed to save themselves and the various stories of hull-walking and swimming for wreckage or launch were described. Yet, it seems probable, one member of the court knew how the launch came to be released; certainly one of the survivors did; and a ship's doctor in HMS *Monarch* also knew. Mr May too, was aware of an incident that was never mentioned in the court proceedings.

According to May, in his personal and later account of the disaster, published in 1872, the launch was free to float because its lashings had been left undone inadvertently earlier in the day when the men securing them were called away to shorten sail. This was related to May, he said, by a survivor in the middle watch who had also been on duty with the same watch from noon until 4 p.m.

May said nothing about this at the court martial but it must be said that there is the possibility that he was told about the lashings after the court martial.

None of the senior officers in the court who, of course, would have been very familiar with ships' boats procedures, thought fit, apparently, to raise the matter.

That anything further is known about it at all is entirely due to an extra-ordinary coincidence that followed publication in 1963 of the first full length book on the loss of the *Captain.*

A copy of the book found its way to a small public library in a South African village called Grabouw on the Palmiet River in the district of Elgin, Cape Province. There it was seen and read by Miss Kathleen Murray. Miss Murray, who died in 1984 at the age of 92, was South Africa's "best woman farmer", to quote Mrs Tini Vorster, wife of the

Republic's former prime minister. She was renowned internationally as a grower of prize winning apples, an enterprise which she started with £25 and one helper when she was 23.

Miss Murray's surprise at seeing the book can be imagined because she had known about HMS *Captain* all her life. She was the youngest daughter of the junior ship's surgeon in HMS *Monarch*; and she was naturally very interested in the account of the disaster since her father, in April 1914, had written his own recollection of the night in the form of a contribution to a private family history which his daughters were compiling as "A Chronicle of the Family."

Dr Murray was a member of a small search party from the *Monarch* which had been ordered by the fleet Admiral to look along the Spanish coast near Finisterre for survivors. Captain John Edmund Commerell, V.C., accompanied the party in two cutters with Lieutenant Arundel and Dr Murray. It seemed to be a forlorn hope that anyone had survived but the party's enquiries along the coast on foot and by mule led them to find May and his men at Corcubion.

Dr Murray wrote, for his daughters' family record:

"The history of how the launch got afloat we heard from another of the survivors. It was a very large launch and was stowed on the *Captain*'s spar deck, resting in great crutches to which it was firmly lashed; fitted with mast, oars etc and covered with stout tarpaulin, it looked one firm solid mass. The narrator told us how, on being relieved from the *first watch* (author's italics), he had been so much alarmed at the condition of the ship that he hesitated to go below, and it occurred to him to cut the lashings of the boat and get into her; he said that he realised that in doing this he was liable to be tried by court martial, but the circumstances seemed to him to justify the risk. No sooner had he accomplished this and got into the boat, than a heavy sea struck the unfortunate ship. She turned right over and the launch was flung into the sea."

Gunner May also disclosed, in his personal narrative, that only one of the survivors, a man who could *not swim*, had *not* been in the sea. He said that this man was Thomas Kernan: and it is quite clear that Kernan was the un-named 'narrator' referred to by Dr Murray.

Kernan gave evidence at the court martial with all the other survivors but, unlike most of them, he was not asked how he managed to escape: however, this may not be significant because neither was the question put to two other young seamen, 19-year-old Robert Tomlinson and 20-year-old Henry Grange. All other survivors, including two 17-year-old Boy seamen, were asked about their escapes.

It is difficult to avoid the suspicion that Kernan was 'protected' during the court martial. He was the 15th witness and was asked by the

146

President, simply:
  What is your age?
  Kernan: 21 years.
  President: How long have you been at sea?
  Kernan: Six years.
  President: You heard the statement of Mr May, the Gunner, read to the court. Have you anything to add to that statement bearing upon the loss of the *Captain*?
  Kernan: Nothing whatever.

Whether Kernan's admission to Dr Murray was a confidence, or whether he spoke openly of his good fortune and, incidental to it, his misconduct in releasing the launch lashings without orders and before the emergency arose cannot be known. From the way Dr Murray recalled the account given by Kernan – "The narrator told *us* . . ." it would seem to have been said openly in the presence of two or more of the search party; perhaps an almost involuntary outpouring of his guilty secret when authority in the person of Captain Commerell, Dr Murray and Lieutenant Arundel came upon the scene.

However it may have been, it is clear that at least one officer and perhaps others knew the truth of the launch's floating free from the sinking ship. Why then, was this matter not probed at the court martial? Was it decided among the admirals that no good would be served by charging Kernan with a naval offence that had resulted in saving the lives of 18 men?

Such a high level conspiracy may not have taken place; but it is quite possible – perhaps even probable – that agonising consideration was given by Captain Commerell to Kernan's inglorious, although understandable and extremely fortunate action in releasing the launch and climbing in: it had not only saved 18 lives but had made it possible for the *Captain*'s last moments to be known and investigated. Ought Kernan to be charged?

In his personal account of the disaster, written after the court martial, Mr May said: "About half past three that afternoon the boom-boats* crews of the watch were piped away to lash and secure the boom-boats but before this could be done the watch was piped to shorten sail which took the men away from securing the boats; and the afternoon watch expiring before sail was taken in, the boats were left unlashed . . . This fact in connection with the boats being left unlashed, I heard from one of my fellow survivors who belonged to the second watch."

---

* Ships boats secured in the deck area where spare spars and booms etc were stored.

Later in his narrative Mr May wrote: "With the exception of one man all the survivors had been overboard and swallowed more or less salt water. This man, Thomas Kernan, got into the launch just as the ship was capsizing and, strange to say, he was the only one in the boat who could not swim."

May was asked during the court martial:

"Do any of the survivors belong to the first watch?"

"None," he replied.

James Ellis, the Gunner's Mate and second senior man in the launch, stated to the court:

"All the men saved belonged to the watch on deck." (i.e. the second or middle watch.)

Ellis volunteered this information in his written statement: May's assertion was in reply to a question. Since Kernan had been in the *first* watch it would seem that both May and Ellis misinformed the court; and they would have to have done so by agreement.

As Dr Murray, and probably Captain Commerell, had heard Kernan's spontaneous confession – that he was one of the first watch and did not want to go below when relieved at midnight – the inescapable inference is that Captain Commerell may have decided that the less said about Kernan's tampering with the launch the better. He would have been well aware of the naval procedure that would follow as soon as they were all safely back in England.

He faced a dilemma: he knew that, inevitably, there would be a court martial to try to find out how the ship came to her end. He had a group of bedraggled sailors who had been through a terrible experience and later they would be examined by a court in a public atmosphere of seething emotion at the loss of so many lives. Was one man to be singled out in ignomony because he had admitted to being afraid and had cut the launch loose, providentially as it turned out? Would it not be equitable enough to conceal the fact that he was the lone survivor from the first watch which went below at midnight; and that, on his own admission he had been first man into the launch before it left the *Captain*'s deck?

If this, or something like it, is what happened then May and Ellis, as the senior survivors, would have had to be made aware of the situation and what was being proposed: they would probably have had no difficulty in accepting the suggestion that it would be for the good of the service not to expose Kernan's misdemeanour. There would appear to have been tacit agreement that Kernan should be lumped in with the other survivors as one of the middle watch on deck at the time of the disaster.

Even if May's later hearsay account of the boats being left unlashed

148

(because more urgent sail shortening took precedence) were true, there is no evidence to deny the possibility – perhaps even likelihood – that the lashings were attended to by the relieving dog watch (divided into two 2-hour watches) some time after 4 p.m. It would have been the duty of the officer in charge of the middle watch to inform his relief of the situation: and, after all, the Admiral was still on board, still inspecting the new ship; every officer would have been keen to avoid sloppiness.

So there is not necessarily any inconsistency between the account given to May by one of the survivors and the facts related by Kernan to Dr Murray and others in Corcubion.

Although there may not have been any wider conspiracy among members of the court, Captain Commerell would have been bound to explain the situation to Admiral Sir Alexander Milne when he reported to the flagship.

Whether the 'protection' of Kernan came about in this way, or however it did, it can be assumed that neither the Admiralty nor the Government expected to lay any blame for the ship's loss on the survivors, they being without exception simple seamen of varying grades and experience. Mr May, although a trained seaman, was a gunner and not responsible for navigation or ship handling. There was no scapegoat among the survivors and in the emotional aftermath that swept the country following the sinking, they were seen simply by everyone as brave British sailors whom Fate had singled out for survival; as indeed they were.

Kernan's real role would have been a positive embarrassment that could have impeached the integrity of the survivors. So the fact that one man was already in the tarpaulin covered launch before it left the ship never emerged at the court martial. Whether Kernan's presence in the launch was noticed by Tregenna when he climbed in from the sea – apparently first man in – and cut away the cover is another unknown factor. He could easily not have noticed Kernan since it was pitch dark in a raging sea and he was struggling for his life. By the time the cover was off and others had dragged themselves in, the earlier presence on board of Thomas Kernan could easily have been entirely unknown to all the rest.

If Kernan's presence in the launch before the ship capsized had been revealed in court – even in the innocent way in which May described it in his later narrative – one of the court must have questioned the fact.

Tregenna and Dryburgh – the hull walkers – had had to tear and cut their way into the launch and it took only a minute or two for the *Captain* to topple on her side.

Lewis Werry said the launch was already floating as he was struggling forward to cut the sails loose. No man on deck in a gale in a capsizing ship would have had time to get into the tarpaulin covered launch in such circumstances; and it could not have been mentioned in court without the incident being queried by experienced seamen.

It may seem curious that Dr Murray, some 40 years after the disaster, did not identify Kernan by name in his contribution to the family history. He must have been privy to any arrangement to conceal Kernan's part in the launch's floating free and perhaps he was still keeping the secret, even from a private family document. Only his daughter's action in sending the doctor's account to the author has given it wider currency.

Another of Dr Murray's recollections of the fatal night was the presentiment of disaster experienced by the veteran ship's Paymaster, Joseph Martin, who had been 27 years in the Royal Navy.

Dr Murray recalled: "Our ship, the *Monarch*, had made ready for the storm – all sails taken in – the topsail yards lowered – the topgallant and royal yards down – steam up – all her boilers ready – her turrets closed up and the guns tarpaulined.

"In fact, she was then much in the same condition in which she would have been if going into action, and into action she did go that night. About midnight the gale raged fiercely and the good old *Monarch* groaned and kicked about and quivered as the heavy seas struck her, each blow being followed by a venomous hissing sound as the water surged past her turrets ... At 12 o'clock I awoke and, curious to see what was going on, went up the hatch and peered out, holding on tight. What a sight it was! ... It must have been about ten minutes past twelve when I stood on the hatchway. I heard the engine-room bell ring and from the bridge, out of pitch darkness, came the voice of Captain Commerell, V.C., in sharp and decisive tone, giving the order to go 'full steam ahead.'

"I went to the wardroom just before breakfast and there I found the Paymaster and Staff Surgeon, in close confab. They looked troubled and the old Paymaster positively ill. I said: 'What's the matter?' He replied: 'Well, I have had a bad night and a horrible dream: I dreamt we had a terrific storm and, in the blackness and turmoil of it all, I saw the *Captain* turn right over. I saw her lying bottom upwards and heard the most awful roar, mingled with shouts of her men as she disappeared ...' At that moment the Lieutenant of the morning watch came in and said: 'The *Captain*'s missing.' during the day the *Helicon* signalled she had passed a boat bottom up and, further on, two dead bodies ... As the day wore on some wreckage, a part of the *Captain*'s bowsprit, was found and, tied on it, a sailor's long silk scarf. Towards evening was found a piece of panelling, painted ebony and gold. It was recognised as belonging to Captain Burgoyne's cabin."

Dr Murray gave no further information about the night of the *Captain*'s loss; but, of course, he had unwittingly called into question the previously accepted evidence of May and Ellis. His written clues to the cover-up lay unknown in the family chronicle until 1966 when Miss Murray thought her father's recollections might interest the author and sent him a copy.

His disclosure of Paymaster Joseph Martin's strange dream of disaster is of interest although it is not possible to deduce exactly when the dream occurred: was it before, during or after the *Captain* went down? What is certain is that Martin had no knowledge of the *Captain*'s capsizing – except his dream – until the lieutenant of the morning watch brought the news that she was missing from the fleet. So the dream perhaps is in the realm of extra-sensory perception: and it was not the only premonition of the *Captain*'s fate that emerged afterwards.

Captain Coles also experienced some kind of foreboding of the disaster which he disclosed to an old naval and family friend, James Whicher, Deputy Inspector-General of the Fleet, a medical rank no longer in use today.

Whicher was also destined to die tragically eight years later – of "Malta Fever" – before he could take up his newly promoted rank of Inspector-General, equivalent to Vice-Admiral.

He and Coles had known each other for many years, probably from boyhood, since Coles's father was the vicar at Ditcham Park and the Whicher family were local landowners with a family medical tradition; they were also related.

Coles spent his last evening ashore in England with the Whicher family at Languard, Southsea. James Whicher congratulated Coles in having, at last, after the years of struggle and perseverance against Whitehall, got the Admiralty to build and commission the ship.

Coles's reply was strangely prophetic as he acknowledged the warm sentiments of his old friend's remark: "Yes, that is true; she is floated at last but I have a strong feeling that in some way she will be the death of me yet."

Mr May recorded other sensations of looming tragedy. One member of the *Captain*'s crew wrote home from Gibraltar about 14 days before the disaster "to the effect that he would never see them again." This was told to May by the wife of a clergyman "who lost a dear son in the vessel."

May also knew of several instances of people in England with relatives or friends in the *Captain* who "were disturbed in their sleep by a variety of causes at or about the time the ship was going down; and one remarkable case was that of a lady who spent many hours of that fearful night weeping and could not assign any other reason for her disturbed state of mind; she was the mother of a very good young man, a sub lieutenant on board the ship and one of the lost ones."

The sleep of otherwise healthy people may be disturbed by a number of temporary physical or emotional influences, not necessarily connected with the death of a loved one: but there have been many instances of people becoming aware of a sudden death or other dramatic incident of which they otherwise had no prior knowledge. The premonitions and unexplained perceptions of death experienced by relatives of the *Captain*'s crew are no more than additions to the history of such phenomena which will continue to attract believers and sceptics for as long as humankind exists: but they happened.

Thomas Kernan, who also had the unusual forename Augustine, went on to have an unblemished career in the navy. Born at Seasalter, near Whitstable, in Kent in 1850, he had joined the navy as a Boy on 12 April 1865 and was four and a half years in his first ship, the *Pallas* until being posted to the *Captain* on 10 October 1869. After the court martial he joined HMS *Bristol* as Acting Seaman Gunner and 14 months later was promoted to Able Bodied rank.

He served in several other ships, reaching the rank of Leading Seaman in the royal yacht *Victoria and Albert* in which he served from April 1874 to March 1880. During the subsequent ten months he was in HMS *Asia* and qualified as Rigger. He returned to the royal yacht in February 1881 for a four and a half year tour of duty as Rigger and Captain of the Main Top. He received a pension in 1892 when he was 42 and subsequently worked in Portsmouth dockyard as a rigger.

CHAPTER 20

WRANGLE IN WHITEHALL

Almost daily throughout the months of September and October 1870 the Admiralty received offers to raise the *Captain*. There were letters from persons with some claim to knowledge of salvage techniques; others were from cranks. The Admiralty declined them all 'with thanks' on receipt of the first letter, or else sent the would-be salvager a printed questionnaire to complete; and there the matter rested.

Some, of course, were more persistent than others, and even when told by the Admiralty that the ship lay in 900 fathoms – more than a mile down – they still repeated their offers.

One Admiralty note on correspondence of the time is typical of most of it: "Mr J. Macdonald says he has a plan for raising the *Captain*. Mr Macdonald thanked and informed that 'my Lords are not in want of plans.'"

One man offered – despite the 900 fathoms – to raise the ship at his own expense – if the Admiralty would undertake to buy it back from him afterwards. Their Lordships – presumably just in case – refused to enter into any such agreement.

But these things were unknown to the general public. What they did know as soon as the court martial findings were published was that Press and Parliament and government were adjudged responsible for the disaster.

The findings had a mixed reception in some quarters. Certain news-papers and periodicals could conceivably have been embarrassed by their past support for Coles and their attacks on those who opposed his ideas. But newspapers seldom admit that their opinions have been wrong. *The Times*, which had been a leading medium for Captain Coles's personal propaganda and had supported him editorially, made it an occasion for general regret.

"It is a most unhappy and perplexing story. The case against the *Captain* herself as an experiment in naval architecture comes out worse than was ever anticipated. In fact, the question seems to be, not whether the ship was a mistake, but whether she was not a mistake so gross as to carry her condemnation on her very face. When we remember however, that this vessel, now given over to universal reprobation, was, so long as she was afloat, the pride of the squadron and the admiration of all the sailors in the fleet; that every officer and man on board of her entertained unbounded confidence in her qualities, and that even the bitterest adversaries of the principle on which she was constructed never ventured to anticipate her destiny, we may well take the lesson to our hearts, and learn caution and circumspection for the future."

The Times, while admitting no guilt specifically, saw the disaster as a lesson for all; which may have made the burden of error less heavy to bear.

It is evident from a letter, written by the President of the Court, Admiral Sir James Hope, who was also Commander-in-Chief, Portsmouth, that there was not entire agreement among the members of the court on the wording of their findings.

Sir James, as Commander-in-Chief, was entitled to comment on court martial findings in his command when forwarding them to the Admiralty for confirmation. But as, in this case, he was also a member of the court, any dissenting comment he might make would look like an alternative or second opinion; and might also be construed as a breach of the regulations imposing secrecy on the deliberations of a court.

Sir James did, in fact, try to write solely in his role as Commander-in-Chief, when sending the findings to the Admiralty: he did not succeed. He pointed out that as he had been a member of the court his remarks would be free from any personal opinion and be "strictly limited to drawing their Lordships' attention to such of the evidence as bears on the conduct of the officers responsible for the handling of the *Captain* on the night of her loss, a question which finds no place either in the sentence of the court or the remarks annexed to it."

Although the Admiral did little more than repeat certain parts of the evidence given, his own opinion was implicit in the selection he made.

"Captain Burgoyne," he wrote, "was on deck when the ship capsized, dressed in a short reefing jacket, blue trousers and peaked cap, with no waterproof or overcoat; a circumstance that – (in conjunction with the weather, which though rainy and threatening more wind, was not of a character previous to 11.45 p.m. to render necessary the presence on deck of a captain who had been in attendance on his Admiral the greater part of the day) – indicates that he had come on deck very shortly before, possibly aroused either by the officer of the watch (Lieutenant Purdon) or by the lurch which occasioned the Gunner (Mr May) to do so.

"Captain Burgoyne did not wait for the muster of the watch to be completed, but endeavoured to shorten sail, whether immediately he comes on deck or otherwise does not appear in evidence . . .

"There is little or nothing in the evidence to show that the direction contained in the Instructions for Lieutenants, 'that every precaution necessary is to be taken to prevent accident from squalls or sudden gusts of wind', had been attended to at all – much to show the reverse, and that the first watch had gone below before they were relieved."

This letter was received with some displeasure at the Admiralty. Their Lordships, although somewhat dismayed at the extent of the court's comments, nevertheless frowned on this supplementary finding – or minority report by the Admiral.

Mr Vernon Lushington, Secretary to the Admiralty at this time, wrote a long minute for the Board, giving his own opinions in the matter for their guidance. He thought the fact that Sir James Hope had commented at all, since he had been a member of the court, was "undesirable."

Sir James's letter "suggests unmistakably and was framed to suggest:

"(a) That either the officer of the first watch had negligently failed to call Captain Burgoyne's attention to the worsening weather; or that Captain Burgoyne, having been called, negligently failed to come on deck immediately, or that he negligently or erroneously omitted to shorten sail.

"(b) That there had been negligence in not establishing the proper and usual system of precautions against squalls; and probably that there was negligence in this respect on the part of the officer of the watch.

"(c) That the first watch was improperly allowed to go below before it was relieved by the middle watch.

"(d) That from these causes rather than from lack of stability the ship was lost.

"Was Admiral Hope justified in offering statements containing such suggestions? This depends partly upon the duties imposed on the court martial.

"I cannot myself doubt that the question of 'the handling of the ship' or, in other words, the conduct of Captain Burgoyne and other officers, who were afterwards drowned, was not merely germane to the enquiry which the court were ordered to conduct – namely as to 'the cause of the loss of the ship' – but that it was a very important part of that enquiry.

"I consider it much to be regretted that the court did not expressly find either that the ship, so far as appeared, was properly handled in all respects before the loss, or that in other (specified) respects she was not properly handled, and that this did, or did not, contribute to her loss. The statement in the finding on this head is not satisfactory.

"It says 'that HMS *Captain* was capsized on the morning of the 7th September 1870, by pressure of sail, assisted by the heave of the sea, and that the sail carried at the time of her loss (regard being had to the force of the wind and the state of the sea) was insufficient to have endangered a ship endued with a proper amount of stability.'

"This proves, on examination, to lead to no certain conclusion. The first impression is that the court thought the ship was properly handled in all respects; but in the end the silence of the finding leaves us uncertain whether in the opinion of the court Captain Burgoyne and the officer of the watch ought not, in the exercise of ordinary skill and caution, to have shortened sail in the first watch; and whether hands should not have been stationed by the topsail sheets and halliards, and these to have been let go at the first sign of the squall which capsized the ship, and whether, if these things had been done, the ship might not have escaped, notwithstanding her insecurity by reason of her small stability.

"I cannot tell why, with such evidence before them as that referred to in Admiral Hope's letter, the court omitted to record their opinion of these, and some other points of the same nature; and especially why they omitted to do so when their President was apparently so fully alive to the importance of these very questions.

"My conjecture is that the court thought they had to try the survivors and not the deceased officers, and that they would not be justified in expressing any opinion on the conduct of the latter.

"If this was the case, or indeed whatever was the reason which operated on their minds, they misunderstood their instructions and committed a mistake which forms a serious flaw in the result of their enquiry.

"They had to enquire into the 'cause of loss', but this they could not do without going fully into all the circumstances immediately preceding the accident, and passing judgment upon the conduct of the persons concerned. They should have carried out their instructions whatever the consequences.

"It is an extremely common thing for legal tribunals (coroners' inquests and other courts of justice) to have, incidentally, to judge the dead. Such a duty fell upon this court martial, but only for the purpose of ascertaining and declaring the 'cause of loss'.

"It appears not improbable that Admiral Hope did endeavour to induce the court to express an opinion on the handling of the ship, and that he was overruled. It may, however, be that he now anticipates that the Admiralty may express its dissatisfaction with the court for their omission in this respect, and that he has written this letter with a view to save himself from any share of the censure.

"If this were so, the letter could not be viewed without some displeasure, as it would appear to be indirectly disclosing his vote or opinion at the court martial. But it may be safely concluded, I think, that Admiral Hope, in writing the letter, was actuated by public motives only, and that he simply desired, as Commander-in-Chief, to call the attention of their Lordships to a point of importance on which the court had expressed no finding.

"Even so, the letter was not, I think, an act of good discretion."

The Board of Admiralty agreed with Lushington's vacillating Whitehallese and adopted the view that he intended them to adopt in spite of his escape clauses: the Board sent Admiral Hope a letter that was something of a rebuff. Their Lordships were of opinion that his letter was "not warranted by precedent, and that if they were to admit it, they would be unable, in any important trials hereafter, to appoint an officer holding the position of Commander-in-Chief to be President of a court martial. Having taken this view of your letter, their Lordships refrain from offering any further observations upon the substance of your remarks."

Sir Spencer Robinson, Controller of the Navy, probably saw in the findings some reflection upon his department, for he also wrote to the Admiralty as soon as he knew of the court's verdict.

"My judgment on the proximate cause of the loss of the *Captain*," he wrote, "founded on the evidence I have read and on my knowledge of the facts, is as follows: On the night of the 7th September the *Captain* was carrying an amount of sail dangerous to a ship of her peculiar construction. Some of the ships of ordinary construction had taken in a third reef in their topsails, others had their topsails lowered on the cap; and before midnight squalls had been experienced and the glass was falling; yet the *Captain*, the ship most liable to danger from heavy squalls, was under double-reefed topsails."

Robinson pointed out that the ship was also heeling more than usual on the afternoon that Admiral Milne was on board and that there was also limited room for handling the sails. There was need for caution during the night and although both Captain Coles and Captain Burgoyne had been warned repeatedly about the danger when the side of the deck met the water, particular caution appeared not to have been taken.

"Instead of caution we find the reverse. Notwithstanding facts which must have been self-evident to every seaman; notwithstanding warnings from the opponents of the design as well as from its promoters; notwithstanding the impression which officers in the fleet derived from remarks made by Captain Coles and Captain Burgoyne that neither of these officers thought the ship beyond a certain point safe under sail, no ship could have been less cautiously handled than the unfortunate

Captain on the night of her loss . . . No doubt anxiety to make the best of the *Captain* led to the imprudence which ended in her loss, but faulty as the ship was, the evidence before the court martial and the facts of the case showed that in all probability, due caution on the part of those on board would have saved her."

This official assessment of the cause of the disaster was in sharp contrast to that of serving officers and friends of the dead men. Captain Sherard Osborn, who had so seriously warned Coles before the first cruise, wrote forcefully to *The Times*:

"Mr Robinson, the master shipwright and engineer, speaks of a report on the stability being completed on August 23rd – a fortnight mark, before the ship was capsized . . . Admiral Sir Alexander Milne tells us that when he expressed alarm to Captain Coles of the extent to which they were pressing the *Captain* on the 6th September Captain Coles pointed to a certain angle as her safe point of inclination, while we now know that the Controller's Department, as early as the 23rd August, possessed mathematical proof that it was utterly erroneous.

"Between that 23rd August and the fatal night on which she and her gallant crew perished there was ample time to have put everyone concerned in testing so novel a form of warship on their guard and, as Captain Commerell of the *Monarch* justly pointed out, had the information proffered to the court martial been put earlier into his or any other senior officer's hands such a catastrophe would have been in all probability averted.

"Mr Reed, the late Chief Constructor, in his evidence leads it to be inferred, if he does not actually say so, that official caution of the stability of a ship, although given under Admiralty seal, would have been treated with indifference or incredulity. In this I totally disagree, and had he been brought up as a naval officer he would know that, as a profession, the tendency is quite in a contrary direction. If he meant that Captain Coles or Captain Burgoyne would have attached very little weight to his own opinion, unsupported by data or mathematical demonstration of the seaworthiness of a low freeboard ship, I think he is right, and he would find hundreds – and I among others – to their way of thinking. Mr Reed and Sir Spencer Robinson have produced too many melancholy failures in the shape of men-of-war for the service to consider them oracles . . .

"I always knew Captain Burgoyne to be as watchful as he was an expert seaman, and most able officer. Blessed with great nerve and calmness, he was never foolhardy, and with such a high sense of responsibility towards those under his command and care that, much as he would have striven to satisfy Captain Coles of his ship's qualities having been fairly developed, he would have been the last man in the Navy to treat with indifference any official and unbiased intimation, had it been given to him, of the sad lack of stability of the *Captain* after she had passed a certain point of inclination under sail.

"It was the withholding of that information, now that we find it was in the possession of certain parties, which I maintain requires the strictest inquiry."

Parliament was in recess throughout the whole of these events. It had risen for the summer on 10 August and did not sit again until 9 February 1871. In the meantime the government, and First Lord of the Admiralty, Hugh Childers, were facing strong criticism.

The First Lord issued a holding statement to the Press announcing that he was "personally engaged in a searching investigation" into the whole history of the building of the *Captain* and that he would publish the results of his inquiries.

The Board of Admiralty did not accept the court's verdict without comment either. A naval court martial was not legally liable to revision. If a sentence happened to be illegal it was not carried out, but the court was always dissolved as soon as the sentence was pronounced and the members of the court were not liable to be censured for any sentence passed by them. The sentence was always that of the majority but each member was, and is, bound by an oath never to reveal the opinion he may have held or the vote he may have cast.

In the sensational trials of Admiral Byng and Lord Keppel, Parliament was asked to sanction the release of the members of the courts martial concerned from their oaths of secrecy. But Parliament has always refused to allow this. If a sentence were illegal it was usual for the Admiralty to point out the fact to the President of the court, and tell him why the sentence could not be carried out. There was no precedent for the Minute which the Board of Admiralty sent to Admiral Sir James Hope on 15 November 1870, having already disposed of his earlier letter to them.

In this second communication their Lordships "express their surprise" at the court's use of the words "a proper amount of stability", without fully explaining what they meant, since it was well known that stability differed as between high- and low-sided ships.

Adopting Lushington's point about whether or not the ship was being prudently handled, they regretted that the court was unable to state more precisely whether the *Captain* was or was not unduly pressed with sail; and "their extreme surprise that so grave a reflection upon 'public opinion', upon 'Parliament' and upon the Board of Admiralty, which in 1866–7 ordered the building of this ship, should have been recorded by a court martial which omitted to examine any member or secretary of either the present or late Boards of Admiralty, or even the officer who then, as now, held the appointment of Controller of the Navy. Thus the 'conviction' which the court martial has felt it necessary to record as to the motives of Parliament and the Board of Admiralty, in failing to comply with the views of the Controller and his Department, is based on the evidence given by two subordinates of that department, and by the late Constructor of the Navy."

The Board went on to say that these omissions would be corrected by the Minute then in course of preparation.

As part of his investigation into the history of the building of the *Captain*, the First Lord asked the Controller, Sir Spencer Robinson, to report on the inclining experiment to find the exact centre of gravity, and the reason for its delay.

In his report the Controller said that, judging after the event, a serious amount of neglect had been imputed to his department for not recommending the Admiralty to detain the ship until the inclining experiment had been made. But he pointed out, rightly, that "this application was made on the ground that it was an interesting piece of statistical science to obtain, apparently rather for the purpose of comparison with certain ships already subjected to such experiment, and not at all on the ground of any doubt or hesitation upon the part of the builders as to their knowledge (by calculation) of the approximate position of the centre of gravity.

"It was, of course, the duty of Messrs Laird to ascertain this and all other particulars to which their attention had been called when their design was accepted; and they assured the Admiralty that their most careful consideration had been given to it. They neither urged nor repeated their application for this experiment, which requires a fine day and a cessation of all work for its success.

"Hitherto there had always been sufficient confidence in the calculations of the approximate position of the centre of gravity and other particulars which the Admiralty designers, and all others, must make as a matter of course, to render it unnecessary to detain ships when required to go to sea.

"The vessels are sent to sea, and upon a convenient opportunity offering, these details are ascertained by actual measurement, and all the ships referred to by Messrs Laird in their application, or ships of the same design, had gone to sea before these measurements were made. In some instances they were not made until the ships had been at sea for many months.

"The *Captain* was treated exactly as all other ironclad ships have been treated in this respect: the experiment was tried on her as it was tried on other ships, when the requirements of the service and the state of work in the Controller's department combined to make it feasible to do so."

Sir Spencer Robinson pointed out that as a result of the experiment it was found that the centre of gravity was about what was usually aimed for in an ironclad ship. Such a position was a happy medium: not too much stability so as to cause excessive rolling; and not too little. But, naturally, such calculation depended on a ship's having a sufficiently high side.

As there was nothing remarkable about the position of the *Captain*'s centre of gravity the Controller said that she would have been allowed to go to sea anyway with no more warning as to the risk of carrying sail on a ship of her lowness of side than had already been given to Captain Coles and Captain Burgoyne by her designers, by Captain Sherard Osborn, and by the papers published and discussed with reference to this very subject.

The calculations as to the ship's stability were based, when first submitted to the Controller on 23 August, on the unlikely event of the ship's forecastle and poop being destroyed so as to give no help in stability. Sir Spencer Robinson said that as he needed to be absolutely sure of his facts and calculations if he were to criticise a ship that had been so favourably reported on at sea, he ordered the calculations to be worked out again on the assumption that the ship was undamaged.

They were still incomplete when the ship went down, but the Controller had been awaiting them "without anxiety, feeling perfectly certain, from what had already been ascertained and reported respecting the *Captain*, that the ship would never be allowed permanently to immerse her lee gunwale, and that nobody would ever have contemplated such an imprudent or ignorant action."

Clearly, Sir Spencer Robinson felt no personal responsibility for the disaster.

The First Lord's dislike of E. J. Reed, which had become almost obsessional during the latter part of Reed's service, seemed, on the loss of the *Captain*, to be transferred to Sir Spencer Robinson, who had already protested to him about his attitude towards Reed. Raised voices and warm exchanges became almost a regular feature in the conduct of high Admiralty business in the First Lord's room.

Reed had only hinted at the feud between himself and Childers in his evidence before the court martial, but it was confirmed by Sir Spencer Robinson in his open conflict with the First Lord which followed.

There can be no doubt that the First Lord's distress at the loss he had suffered in the death of Leonard, his midshipman son, was almost more than he could bear. Assailed by self-reproach at having personally secured the boy's transfer from the *Monarch* to the *Captain* – demonstrating his small opinion of Reed and his regard for Coles

– Childers must have seen in Sir Spencer Robinson the instrument of his grief, the man who appeared to have known the danger, but yet had given no further specific warning of it.

On 14 December he saw Robinson in his room at the Admiralty and, according to Childers, who wrote a memorandum to Prime Minister W.E. Gladstone about it, the Controller agreed at this private face-to-face meeting to resign at the end of his 10-year term of office, due to be completed on 7 February 1871.

This 'request' for retirement from the First Lord was in sharp contrast to the lavish encomium given to Robinson by both Childers and the prime minister the previous summer, when the Controller was considering resignation; they persuaded him to carry on.

The day after the Childers–Robinson encounter at the Admiralty, the substance of which Robinson flatly denied, the First Lord published his Minute on the loss of the *Captain.*

The Childers Minute, as it is known, proved to be, in effect, a complete rejection of the court martial's findings and strictures and a defence of the First Lord and of the First Sea Lord, Sir Sydney Dacres. The Minute, together with the printed Admiralty evidence put before the court and various extracts from government publications and correspondence tending to support the First Lord's case, amounted to 359 pages and was laid before Parliament when it reassembled on 9 February 1871.

Whilst formally accepting full responsibility himself for whatever happened in his department, the First Lord claimed, in brief, that the entire responsibility for the completion of the *Captain* as an effective sea-going man-of-war rested on Captain Coles and Lairds, and had been accepted by them; that although this responsibility continued until the ship's trials were completed, the Controller of the Navy necessarily became responsible for her fitness to go to sea; that if he had had any cause to anticipate danger it was his duty to say so; that no such danger had been foreseen and no warning given; and that, in the absence of any warning the First Sea Lord, Sir Sydney Dacres was justified in ordering the ship's trials at sea.

Childers also said that the experiment to find the position of the centre of gravity and work out the details of the ship's stability should not have been so long delayed; and finally, that the Controller, on receiving the report on the *Captain*'s stability on 23 August, ought to have called special attention to it, and to have recommended that it should be passed on to Captain Burgoyne and the Commander-in-Chief of the fleet.

The Minute also announced the formation of a Committee of Designs to inquire whether British warships were being constructed along the right lines – a clear affront to E. J. Reed, the former Chief Constructor.

162

The Minute threw much of the blame upon the Controller who, with Reed, had from the first opposed the idea of a low-sided ship carrying a full sailing rig.

The Controller replied officially to the criticism, which had enraged most naval officers who saw it as further evidence of Childers' reputation in the service for being an autocratic minister, notoriously overbearing towards his subordinates. His Minute was regarded in the navy as unjust to the Controller and his department and no credit to Childers himself.

In his reply, which at his request was also laid before Parliament, Sir Spencer Robinson disclaimed all responsibility for the success or failure, safety or danger of the *Captain*. The objections to the ship had been stated by the department, but no imminent danger was foreseen. In fact, said Sir Spencer, not only was the *Captain considered* safe to go to sea, but she *was* safe if properly handled.

Lairds, he said, should have established the position of the centre of gravity before the ship left their yard. They had never expressed any doubt about her stability, and the *Captain* was treated, in this respect, like any other ironclad; the experiment was carried out when the requirements of the Service permitted. The report of 23 August giving details of her stability after the inclining experiment *was* put before Mr Childers, whose duty it then was, in consultation with the First Sea Lord, to inform the fleet if he thought it necessary.

Early in 1871 Robinson published his correspondence with Gladstone, which made public the disagreement between himself and Childers. If the personal relationship between the First Lord and the Controller had been somewhat delicate before, this exposure of their enmity towards each other meant that one of them had to go.

Childers, a close friend and something of a protegé of Gladstone, was abroad at this time, trying to restore his health which had deteriorated during the agony of the preceding months. It was left to Gladstone to insist upon Sir Spencer Robinson's departure from the Admiralty.

Throughout a lengthy and formal correspondence with the prime minister, Robinson insisted to the end that he had never agreed to resign, that Childers's account of their interview was false and, in view of the public attack on him by the First Lord, he never would resign.

"It is painful to me to be obliged to refer to the melancholy loss of the *Captain*," he wrote to Gladstone, "as the real cause of Mr Childers's desire to remove me from my present position. Mr Childers, in common with a number of gentlemen in and out of Parliament, and supported by several naval officers, was a firm believer in Captain Coles and a strenuous advocate of his system: he disregarded such warnings as he received of the risk incurred by this mode of construction, and when the unfortunate catastrophe to the *Captain* occurred, his endeavours were directed to throw the blame which might be supposed to attach to himself – for the great encouragement he had given Captain Coles – on those who had throughout expressed their disapproval of such methods of construction.

"The peculiarly hostile relations which he had established with Mr Reed disturbed his judgment, as I frankly told him, and induced him to suppose that, by promoting an attack on the naval construction directed by that gentleman, he could divert the attention of the public and Parliament from the loss of the *Captain* and from the bias he had always shown to Captain Coles. I should be unfit for the position I hold had I not stated strongly my objections to the course Mr Childers intended to follow, and to the appointment of the committee he proposed.

"He disregarded my opinion and although, under other circumstances, I should probably have left office, this case was so important I felt it my duty, at any sacrifice, to endeavour to render the results as little injurious to the public service as possible . . ."

Robinson also recalled the publication of the Childers' Minute the day after his meeting with the First Lord at the Admiralty, and the fact that he had not been shown a copy until it was made available to the Press.

Gladstone courteously and skilfully replied to Robinson's letters, saying little except that in view of all that had happened in the Admiralty – and to much of which Robinson had again drawn his attention – a change was necessary.

Robinson retired at the end of his term and was granted a pension in addition to his Admiral's half-pay. On the whole, he comes out of the correspondence with conviction and dignity.

The loss of the *Captain* sounded the tocsin for any lingering support for the idea of persevering with the principle of a low-sided, fully-rigged ocean-going warship. The Committee of Designs, when it reported, turned out to be to some extent an endorsement of Reed's professional opinions and reassured the public concerning the safety of the *Devastation*, the Reed-designed mastless, steam turret ship, then being built, which may be considered to be the forerunner of battleships as they developed in the following decades into the 20th century.

The committee said that if the *Captain* had floated with 8 feet of free-board, as designed, she would have been "comparatively safe" under canvas. But, even then, her "range of stability" – the difference between two angles of heel under sail; the first, at which the righting force was at its maximum, and the second, where the ability to recover vanished – was too narrow a margin of safety unless such extreme care was taken not to tilt the ship too far over as to be "unprecedented in the rules and usages of seamanship as applied to decked vessels." In other words, she would have been "comparatively safe" if carefully nursed; which, obviously, would be a liability in any ship of war.

Comparing the *Monarch* with the *Captain* (as designed, not as she actually floated) "the committee calculate that the greatest angle at which it is safe to sail the *Monarch* at a steady heel to be 13¾° and the similar angle for the *Captain* to be 4½°."

Two admirals on the committee declined to sign the main report and complained that out of the committee of 16 only 6 were naval officers. They were Admiral George Elliot and Rear-Admiral Alfred Ryder, who submitted their own minority report.

Their detailed dissent went into considerable technical detail which is outside the scope of this book; but they showed naval men's support for Captain Coles's idea. They pointed out that the *Captain* design, *as a type*, was not dangerous if built to float with adequate freeboard: the trouble with the *Captain* had been that too much weight was built into her. It was this, of course, that had concerned the Admiralty observers throughout the ship's building. But Admirals Elliot and Ryder made their point that Captain Coles's idea was all right but it had been put into practice wrongly.

They made no criticism of the navy Constructor's Department but could not resist a sailor's comment on ship designers: "Members of the Constructor's Department should have some experience *at sea* . . . We believe they would cordially welcome the prospect. One of them should always be in the Mediterranean flagship, another in the Channel Fleet flagship. A cruise for three months in the Channel Fleet in the winter months might advantageously precede promotion. It is difficult to suppose that it would not be very beneficial for the public service if these gentlemen witnessed personally at sea the effect of wind and waves, sail &c upon the fabrics they have to design and construct."

Childers resigned as First Lord through ill health in March 1871, but after some months on the Continent he recovered sufficiently to take office again in 1872. He subsequently had a distinguished career in Parliament and business. He died in January 1896.

Where then, in this story of endeavour and disaster, does the blame lie? Captain Coles was a man whose brilliance on this occasion was misconstrued: E. J. Reed (later Sir Edward) – who went on to a notable career as a private shipbuilder, author and Member of Parliament – cannot be blamed for having been right, although it is probable that he was more right than he at first supposed, or he must else have protested formally at the ship's going to sea.

The same assessment must be made of his superior, Vice-Admiral Sir

Spencer Robinson, Controller of the Navy. Childers was a politician who mistakenly disregarded his professional advisers, partly perhaps because of his lack of regard for them; although when the extent of the public support for Coles is considered, the First Lord's error of judgment – tragic for himself – may be understood.

No evidence survived of the state of the *Captain*'s trim on the night she went down: but the evidence of Admiral Sir Alexander Milne that the lee edge of the deck was permanently awash during the afternoon does show that the ship was heeling over more that day than was usual, even if it did not alarm Captain Coles.

Was she lighter, through consumption of fuel and stores, and therefore exerting fewer foot-tons of resistance to the pressure of the wind on the sails? And was this because water ballast had not been let into her double bottom provided to adjust the trim and bottom weight?

These facts can never be known: but the fact that she *was* being sailed with the lee gunwale in the sea showed either ignorance on the part of Burgoyne and Coles of the widely known danger involved – which is inconceivable; or recklessness, which is unlikely on Burgoyne's record.

The answer seems to be that their practical sailing experience in the ship – which had seemed to deny all the misgivings about sails and low freeboard – had given them a dangerous confidence in her as an *individual* vessel in spite of her type. They did not have the doom-laden scientific evidence against her; and they thought, notwithstanding all the Jeremiahs, that she was all right.

Which is what the court martial, in effect, found.

CHAPTER 21

THE ADMIRAL AND THE DEAN

Within a month of the disaster a major distress fund had been set up. Queen Victoria gave £100 – about £4000 in today's money – and Edward, Prince of Wales, gave an appropriately lower sum proportionate to his rank, of 50 guineas. Donations, from shillings to pounds, came in from all over the country; and local committees were formed to organise collections. One poignant contribution of five shillings – about £10 today – came from "the mother of one who perished in HMS *Racehorse*", recalling a previous loss.

Orphanages, homes and schools offered free places to *Captain* orphans; army officers stationed at Woolwich put on a stage show; and a West End theatre gave a morning performance, the actors appearing without pay, to raise £100 for the fund.

As the months passed and the erstwhile supporters of Captain Coles played out their lengthy game of pass-the-parcel with the responsibility for the ship having been built, those whose connection with the *Captain* had been of a closer and more emotional nature were beginning to consider how best to commemorate the great loss of life.

A committee was formed at a large meeting held on 18 July 1872 at the Royal United Services Institute in its historic Whitehall building; it was here, from a first floor window, that Charles I stepped out on to the scaffold and his execution.

The building was now again the setting for a sombre purpose as the new First Lord of the Admiralty, George J. Goschen, who was in the chair, said that additional funds beyond what had been raised already were needed to provide a "fitting memorial" to those who died in the disaster. The meeting was not being held to discuss the causes of the *Captain*'s sinking: "Here the voice of controversy is hushed," he said, "and we have all come here – some representing the Navy, some the sister service, as well as representatives of the country at large – anxious to have the opportunity of showing how deeply we feel the great calamity which this country suffered on that terrible night when the ship was lost."

Sir John Elphinstone, M.P., told the meeting that the *Captain* fund already stood at between £50,000 and £60,000 (£2.2–£2.5 million in today's money) and he thought a great deal more could be raised by the new committee, which was to include Admirals George Elliot and Alfred Ryder, the determined dissenters on the Designs Committee. The money raised so far was to help the widows and orphans; but now there was a need for "an enduring monument."

Some fulsome tributes were paid to those lost in the ship who "heroically yielded up their lives." No one, of course, pointed out that their "deeds of heroism" were like the helpless drowning of kittens in a bucket: the hundreds of trapped men had had no more chance or choice in their fate. It would be for the outspoken Dean of Westminster, the Very Reverend Arthur Penrhyn Stanley, to point, as delicately as he could, to this sad but unseemly aspect of the tragedy.

Rear-Admiral Alfred Ryder was the most active member of the committee and he lost no time in writing to potential donors. Lord Northbrook sent £50 – worth about £2000 today – and said he agreed with the committee's decision to instal a stained glass window in Westminster Abbey, commenting, "our artists are better in glass than in stone."

The intention of the committee was to have two memorials in the Abbey, a window and, elsewhere – possibly in the cloister – a brass plaque bearing the names of all those lost in the ship. It was left to Admiral Ryder to negotiate this following a preliminary meeting in Portsmouth between Dean Stanley and some members of the committee.

The Dean, former celebrated Oxford don, eminent ecclesiastical scholar, friend of the Prince of Wales, and married to Lady Augusta Bruce, a daughter of the 7th Earl of Elgin, was custodian of the Abbey for 17 years and was one of Westminster's most intellectual and influential incumbents; as well as having personal charm, so it is said.

Whether Admiral Ryder found him charming may be doubted, as their respective roles put them on a collision course over the *Captain* memorial. Ryder wrote to the Dean, setting out the committee's request, which perhaps had not been explained in full at the Portsmouth meeting.

It is possible that admirals become accustomed to obedience or, at least, ready compliance with their wishes; it is a concomitant of very high rank in any walk of life. So Admiral Ryder was probably not particularly charmed on 12 September 1872 to receive a hurriedly scrawled, almost unreadable letter from the Dean – (a great traveller who was about to leave on one of his regular visits to the Continent) – in which he shied away from the idea of a brass plate bearing *all* the names of the *Captain*'s complement.

The Dean wrote that he had not realised there would be so many names or that the memorial (apart from the stained glass window) would be "on so large a scale": there is no record of the proposed size of the brasses. However, it is quite likely that the Dean's next observation of dissent would have annoyed the Admiral more, as he read:

"The difficulty which I feel is that – (if I have to admit so very elaborate a record of all the persons who perished in the *Captain*, most tragically but not in any great act of heroism or devotion) – I should be doing an injustice both to those who may be commemorated hereafter in the Abbey for actual service rendered to the country . . ."

The Dean said he would like to deliberate further before making a decision. He had to make judgments among the different applications he received for memorials and he could not allow "two memorials of the same event to appear in different parts of the Abbey."

He would decide what to do when he returned to England in the following month. Having written that, the Dean apparently thought that he had gone a bit too far in downgrading the quality of the loss of life in the ship, for he added a postscript: "I hope that you will not misunderstand . . . (illegible . . .) as though I in any way depreciated the irreparable loss to the country of those who perished in the *Captain* or overlooked the fact that they died in the course of their duty as much as if they had fallen in battle . . . I mean that it belongs to a different category of honour; and I have to deal as circumspectly as possible so as to avoid entanglements for the future, as well as to have ample space for posterity."

The Dean was clearly having difficulty in trying to make a distinction between a sailor drowned in his hammock and a sailor shot, perhaps by an unseen sniper, on deck during a sea battle – as Lord Nelson was. If a dispassionate view is taken, there is no difference: a sailor shot down by an unknown marksman and a sailor drowned, trapped as he wakes briefly from his rest below deck, both suffer their deaths involuntarily; as do soldiers advancing under orders towards enemy fire. A life lost thus in time of war occurs while on active service, or in action; in peacetime it is while routinely serving the country; but it is a timeless convention for the death in war to be considered more heroic even though the distinction is seldom, if ever drawn. Naturally, a difference may be seen between a life lost unwittingly in the course of an engagement on land or sea and one lost, or put at great risk, by the personal decision and act of an individual in battle: that, of course, is what distinguishes heroes.

In an Abbey crowded with heroic effigies to the brave of the past Dean Stanley's shuffling of words as he sought to explain the virtually unexplainable may be understood. Whether his semantic softening of attitude mollified Admiral Ryder, or not, there is no knowing; but the Dean's Continental break did nothing to change his stance regarding

169

the proposed dual memorial, and on 20 November 1872 he wrote again to the Admiral.

"I have come to the conclusion that a tablet recording all the names of those who perished in the *Captain* would be so far out of proportion to the records which one would be able to admit, even in the case of the greatest victories, that I do not feel justified in deviating from the usual precedents of the Abbey in agreeing so detailed an enumeration. Of course, if the Government were to urge it and so relieve me of the responsibility, I should gladly acquiesce, but short of some proposal of this kind I feel that I must ask you to confine the memorial to the window, already agreed upon, and to a small tablet on the floor commemorating the principal names and the numbers of those who were lost."

It may be assumed that Admiral Ryder had some private thoughts about the Dean's attitude; but in the absence of any record they can only be imagined. Nevertheless, viewed at a distance and free of the emotion that inevitably surrounded the loss of the *Captain* it is possible to have some understanding of the Dean's dilemma as custodian not only of the Abbey's present but also of its future as a national shrine; creating precedents for posterity to sort out may be not only unwise but irresponsible as well.

Whatever the Admiral thought about this setback at Westminster, he was not in a mood to sail away from these disturbed waters – not far, anyway. With the committee's approval he took the problem a short distance to the east, to St Paul's Cathedral, where England's most famous sailor, Horatio Nelson lies.

The Dean and Chapter of the Cathedral were "very glad to give a place in St Paul's to a memorial to the officers and men whom we lost in the *Captain*." The only provisos were that the memorial brasses should not be Gothic; should "suit the architecture of St Paul's" and "have a distinctly Christian significance."

This preliminary agreement was dated 5 December, only a fortnight after the Dean of Westminster had declined to have this "enumeration of all the names" in the Abbey. It shows that Admiral Ryder was not a man to waste time when there was an objective to be reached. He immediately sent a preliminary design of the memorial to St Paul's and received a reply dated 9 December.

It appears that this first conception of the brasses provided for an engraving across the top with a representation of the Ark and HMS *Captain* in some sort of association. The Dean and his brethren thought this was "hardly the sort of ornament for such a memorial." They did not explain their objection any further but it was presumably thought that the design represented too close a relationship between the ill-fated man-made ship of war and the most famous craft of peace in Christian belief. The Dean and Chapter suggested possible alternatives such as "Our Lord in the storm on the lake" or "St Paul's shipwreck."

The short inscription, as first worded, referred to the crew who "perished" when the ship "capsized". Objection was taken to the use of both these words: "perished" was considered to be "a not very Christian word" and "capsized" was too technical. The Dean and brethren thought "lost" would be a better word than "perished". They pointed out that although the men had been *lost* it was the Christian hope and belief that they had not *perished.*

It was a rather semantic difference between the two sides and after a personal discussion between the Dean and Admiral Ryder a final inscription was agreed as: "In memory of the Officers, Seamen, Marines and Boys who died on September 7th 1870 when HMS *Captain* foundered off Cape Finisterre."

Instead of the Ark and the *Captain* together, the brass was engraved across the top to show HMS *Captain* alone, with no sails rigged, steaming towards a rising sun.

Below this came the controversial finding of the court martial, followed at the bottom by the names of the officers on board.

On a similar brass plaque (which was to be placed opposite the first on the other side of the great black doors in the north wall of the cathedral) were listed the 400-odd complement of seamen, marines and boys who died with the ship.

So the Admiral and his committee got their two memorials, one in each of London's two most famous centres of Christian worship; and they complement one-another.

The big stained window in the North Transept of Westminster Abbey was created in two vertical panels, each panel depicting five scenes with nautical associations from the Bible. The left panel shows: Building of the Ark; Passage through the Red Sea; Fleet of King Solomon; Building the Ship of Tyre; Deliverance of Jonah.

On the right: Christ stills the Tempest; Christ walking on the Sea; Christ teaching from the ship; Miraculous draught of fishes; Shipwreck of St Paul.

Near the window, which without explanation can mean little to an observer, there is a brass panel let into the stone floor. It reads: "The stained window above commemorates the foundering of HMS *Captain* on Sept 7 1870 when Captain Hugh Burgoyne, V.C., Captain Cowper Coles, C.B., with 49 officers and 402 men and boys perished off Cape Finisterre in the service of their country. The names are recorded on brasses in St Paul's Cathedral."

Unfortunately, this panel in the floor is nowadays nearly always concealed by rows of rigidly attached chairs that help to accommodate the large congregations which the Abbey attracts on frequent occasions. It is probable, therefore, that many visitors to Westminster may be unaware of the nature of the window or what it commemorates.

So both Deans also got their way; and very likely the Admiral and his committee got more in the end out of the difference of opinion with Dean Stanley than would have been the case if he had allowed both the window and the brasses to find places in the Abbey: for it may be doubted that such a well connected establishment figure as Dean Stanley would have allowed the court martial's indictment of Parliament, Press and public to be permanently displayed just across the road from the Houses of Parliament and among the Abbey's justly laudatory monuments to the nation's heroes.

CHAPTER 22

IN LINE AHEAD

Even as HMS *Captain* plunged to her final resting place, the triumphant story of Coles's turret was continuing – in ships without sails that, nevertheless, would make the oceans their highways. If the *Devastation* is remembered as the forerunner of subsequent battleship design, she, in turn, had her beginnings in the *Cerberus*, created by E. J. Reed to meet the special requirements of harbour defence in Melbourne, Australia.

So long as the Admiralty had insisted on a sailing rig for sea-going cruisers, Reed had insisted on building with high sides for good stability. But the requirement for harbour defence was different. Freed from the need to incorporate masts and sails in his design, Reed readily accepted the usefulness of a low freeboard.

Not only did low sides mean that a ship rolled less and therefore aided accurate gunfire, but the weight of armour saved by the reduced height of side to be plated meant the weight could be diverted to armour over the decks to protect the ship from dangerous plunging shot.

The *Cerberus*, laid down in September 1867, nine months after the *Captain* was commenced, was completed in September 1870, in which month the *Captain* was lost. *Cerberus* was, in fact, a monitor, and except for the *Captain*, was the first officially constructed ship with a low free-board. Mastless, she had a centrally built superstructure and a turret at each end of it. There was a clear field of fire over the bows from the forward turret, and similar unobstructed fire astern from the after turret. Thus, between them the two turrets could fire in any direction.

The *Cerberus* was also the first British warship to have an armoured wall, or breastwork, rising from the deck and completely surrounding the lower part of the turrets and superstructure. Reed adopted this breastwork because protection was necessary for funnel, turret bases and airshafts. Enclosing everything behind a wall of iron not only gave the necessary protection from gunfire, but kept the turrets, airshafts and hatchways clear of the sea.

In the *Cerberus* is seen the genesis of the design to which all battleships were built from 1885 to 1905 – with the main batteries sited in armoured positions fore and aft, uninterrupted bow and stern fire, and wide arcs of fire on both sides of the ship.

Yet the *Cerberus*, being built for the colonial navy, aroused little interest at home. The usual searching criticism in the technical Press was absent when she was commissioned. One picture and a brief mention was all that the novel little ship received, since she was destined for an unspectacular life in and around a harbour on the other side of the world.

Although the last sea-going battleship to carry a full sailing rig – the *Shannon* – was not to be completed until September 1877, in the meantime, modern battleship design came a stage nearer in the *Devastation*. Designed by Reed and commenced in November 1869, the *Devastation* (modified by Reed's successor, Barnaby) was completed in April 1873. She had twin screws, fore and aft turrets at either end of the amidships superstructure, and she carried a huge supply of coal, necessary for long-distance cruising with the uneconomical steam engines of that time.

Like the *Cerberus*, the *Devastation*'s superstructure and turrets were surrounded by a breastwork of armour. She was, in fact, a somewhat larger version of the *Cerberus*. When Barnaby took over from Reed he modified the ship, notably by bringing the central superstructure out to the edges of the deck and thus virtually increasing the height of the ship's sides: but for all practical purposes she was Reed's ship.

The *Devastation* was not an attractive-looking vessel. She appeared to be top heavy and so far as the sail-loving public were concerned she was committed to the sea with some misgivings. When she was commissioned at Portsmouth a notice was fixed anonymously to her gangway, reading: "Letters for the *Captain* may be posted aboard." With the *Captain* disaster still a vivid public memory, the grim suggestion was plain.

Engine trouble during her first cruise did nothing to increase public confidence, but as her trials proceeded she vindicated the faith of the Admiralty in her design. On trial in a gale with waves running 20–26 feet high, a report on her behaviour said: "A wall of water would appear to rise up in front of the vessel, dashing on board in the most threatening style as though it would carry all before it, rush aft against the fore turret with great violence and, after throwing a cloud of spray off the turret into the air, divide into two, to pass overboard on either side."

On the whole, the *Devastation* proved to roll only modestly and, in fact, her sister ship, the *Thunderer*, was always held up by those who knew her as a model of steadiness. The oft-used phrase "as steady as the old *Thunderer*" became the highest praise for a warship as a gun platform. However, the low freeboard, particularly at the bows, made both ships susceptible to severe head-on seas at speed, and after a taste of bad

Atlantic weather they were restricted to home waters and Mediterranean duties.

In direct line of descent from the *Devastation* was the *Dreadnought*, designed originally by Reed as the *Fury* of 10,460 tons. Building began on 10 September 1870 but was stopped in 1871 pending the report of the Committee on Designs. The hull had been built as far as the armoured main deck, but in view of several recommendations made by the committee Reed's drawings were scrapped and a new set was prepared by Mr W. H. White, a naval architect who had been Reed's confidential secretary, and now held a similar position with Sir Nathaniel Barnaby, Reed's successor.

But basically the *Dreadnought* was a Reed design – and he always claimed her as such. She was the last of the true ironclads, having a hull almost completely covered with what the navy soon called "pie-crust" – armour that was adequate at the time she was designed but was useless against even moderate sized guns by the time she was completed. Thus did guns outstrip armour.

With her overall flat deck – level from stem to stern – her two turrets rising stolidly from it fore and aft of the central superstructure, she lay on the water, big, broad and menacing – the very embodiment of her name. Commissioned in 1879, she remained in service for 25 years to become one of the best-loved ships in the Royal Navy.

The Reed-dominated era of construction in which a central armoured citadel enclosed turrets and vitals of the ship, came to an end with the building of the *Trafalgar*. When this ship was authorized in the Naval Estimates for 1886 the Financial Secretary to the Admiralty, obsessed – as was everyone – with the growing menace of torpedoes in sea warfare, said in the Commons: "I may safely say that these two large ironclads (*Trafalgar* and *Nile*) will probably be the last ironclads of this type that will ever be built in this or any other country."

It was thought that capital ships were sitting ducks for a torpedo boat. But only two years later the First Lord was telling Parliament: "The powers of these torpedo boats had been greatly exaggerated by naval officers. France suspended battleship building and other nations followed her example; but since then, owing in part to the invention of quick-firing guns, there has been a return to the building of battleships."

It was, in fact, to be another 50 years before the capital ship would be eclipsed.

The *Trafalgar*, of 12,500 tons, was the heaviest British warship built so far. She was the last single citadel (i.e. with a single breastwork of armour completely surrounding turrets and superstructure) turret ship to be built, and the first to have a secondary armament of six quick-firing 6-inch guns in addition to the two 13.5-inch guns in each turret. She also mounted eight 6-pounders, nine 3-pounders and had five torpedo tubes.

The tendency among designers by now was to break up the single central citadel into two or more separate armoured areas round the main guns, so as to save the weight of the heavily armoured ship sides which were an essential feature of the central citadel design.

The *Trafalgar* was really built against the wishes of Barnaby and his successor, White, who had been enticed back into Admiralty service, having left it for three years to become the brilliant head of Armstrong's shipbuilding yard. The *Trafalgar* was the first ship built under White's responsibility, her building having been sanctioned about the time he took over from Barnaby.

White – Sir William White as he became – left the mark of his genius on the Fleet during his period as Director of Naval Construction. Both Reed and Barnaby had experimented with different designs without producing an outstanding class of ship to be reproduced in numbers.

Reed's difficulties, owing to the fundamental changes that were taking place in ship design and construction, are known, but he was allowed a certain amount of freedom in his work – more so than any of his successors.

For Barnaby it may be said that he, too, in charge of Admiralty construction for 13 years, had to contend with constantly changing requirements for warships. Armour did not keep pace with gun power, and in addition to the heavy guns in turrets which had determined design hitherto, secondary armaments of smaller guns, giving additional all-round and close range fire, took their place among the heavy guns and added to the designer's problems.

Such great thicknesses of wrought iron and steel were required to keep out the heaviest shot that the sheer weight of it limited the amount that could be used and the areas which could be protected.

But Barnaby was not allowed the same independence that Reed had enjoyed. So if his period of office from 1872 to 1885 is not identified with any outstanding new designs the fault may not have been so much his as that of the Board of Admiralty, who largely dictated what kind of ships he would produce. He also served through a period of government economy during which the Navy was allowed to run down.

Between the years 1873 and 1883, although the cost of individual ships was increasing rapidly, the Naval Estimates were pegged at around £11,000,000 and economy was practised to the extent of a reckless hazarding of Britain's position as a dominant sea power.

Admiral Arthur William Acland Hood – Commander-in-Chief, Channel Fleet, and later First Sea Lord – declared: "We have ships without speed, guns without range, and boilers with only a few months' life in them. This is called economy, but it is really not spending money, closing the purse strings, and keeping our Fleet in such a state of inefficiency and unpreparedness as to render it comparatively useless should we at any time become involved in war with a maritime power."

Barnaby's personal relations with Reed, who became the arch-critic of Admiralty-built ships after he left government service, may also have inhibited Barnaby in creative design. Although Barnaby resigned in July 1885 on the ground of poor health, his grandson has said that the real reason was "he had become tired of the perpetual quarrels with his brother-in-law, Reed, which were making things difficult for family relations. He was very fond of his sister and the two families were close neighbours." In spite of his 'ill health' Barnaby lived to the age of 86. He died in June 1915.

White came to office under an administration that was ready to rejuvenate the Navy. Public concern had been aroused a few months earlier by a series of articles in the *Pall Mall Gazette*, focusing attention on the Fleet's deficiencies in ships, equipment, organisation and personnel.

The *Trafalgar*, although laid down in January 1886, would not be ready for service until March 1890. Meanwhile, in August 1888, White was recalled from holiday and directed to prepare designs for an improved version of *Trafalgar*.

He disagreed with following the same line of construction and after a meeting between the Board of Admiralty, White and some expert senior naval officers, it was decided to adopt White's preference for mounting the big guns in barbettes and not in the cylindrical turrets invented by Coles.

In a barbette the barrel of the gun was fully exposed and it fired over the top of an armoured enclosure behind and below which the gunners, aided by machinery, served the guns – which by now were breech loading. At first barbettes varied in design. Some had no overhead protection for the gunners, simply the wall of armour. Others were enclosed. Later the name reverted to turret; but the barbette principle remained.

A disadvantage of the low freeboard turret ships was that they were unable to steam fast in the open sea. Having low bows to facilitate forward fire from the turret, they took heavy seas on to the foredeck. It was not realized by designers that the height of the bow determined the speed at which a ship could be driven against the sea. Depending, among other things, on the height of the ship's sides, the shape of the bow and state of the sea, when a certain speed is reached so much water comes aboard and head resistance to the ship increases so much that it is impossible to increase speed any further.

Given certain essentials of design by the Board of Admiralty – including barbette gun mountings, a high freeboard and a secondary battery of quick-firing guns to be disposed round the ship – White designed one of the most attractive and successful battleships that had been produced to date in Britain.

The *Royal Sovereign* class, as they were called, were not only mighty in offensive power, but had a ferric beauty of their own. Not for 20 years had the Navy seen such symmetrical, handsome and practical men-of-war. Displacing 14,150 tons and 380 feet long, *Royal Sovereign* mounted four 13.5-inch guns, with the rest of the armament in quick-firers: ten of 6-inch calibre; sixteen 6-pounders; twelve 3-pounders and seven torpedo tubes. She carried a crew of 712 and could steam all out at 18 knots.

The invention of nickel steel armour plate made a big contribution to the design, enabling a reduction in the weight and thickness of armour formerly necessary when only iron had been available. Seven of the class were built, the last being *Royal Oak*, completed in June 1894.

During 1892–93 there was again government reaction against any increase in naval expenditure (i.e. bigger ships), and in naval circles too, there was a body of opinion opposed to the monster guns which dictated to a great extent the size of the ship that had to carry them. There was an agitation for building a greater number of vessels of moderate size and armament instead of a few giant capital ships.

White wrote a memorandum for the Board of Admiralty on this subject; and his arguments have held good for every similar objection made since to sending the largest possible guns to sea.

"The general idea underlying all these proposals," White wrote, "is that even in the largest ships there are considerable areas of the upper works unarmoured, and liable to speedy destruction by shell-fire from guns of moderate calibre, with quick-loading mechanism and high explosives as the bursters. Moreover, the armour extends but a moderate distance below the load-line in still water, and either a moderate angle of roll or change of water level due to wave motion may expose the weak bottom below the armour to perforation by chance projectiles, which would readily find access to the vitals.

"Taking these facts into account, it is urged that there is no need to carry armour-piercing guns of great power, that moderate calibres (9.2-inch or 10-inch at the most) should not be exceeded, and few of these carried. Quick-firing guns of 6-inch calibre and below, it is considered, should form the bulk of the armaments. A moderate number of these should be mounted in one ship in order to diminish the risk of serious loss involved

178

in the destruction of a unit of an attacking force. Since armour protection has the restricted value above described, it is argued that it may be dispensed with, or made very moderate in thickness and extent. In this manner the size and cost of individual ships can be kept within modest limits.

"The capital expenditure on a few large battleships carrying heavy guns in strongly armoured positions, and a great weight of armour on certain portions of their hulls, can be made to produce a considerably greater number of smaller ships, each of which, it is considered, is as efficient against underwater attacks as larger ships. The united action of these smaller ships against the less number of vessels of larger type would, according to the advocates of the former, almost certainly secure their victory . . .

"For many services besides fleet actions – such as covering a stretch of coastline or sweeping an area of sea – the increase in numbers would be of immense value. With larger numbers in a fleet, small squadrons could be detached from the main body without seriously crippling the force. In short, increase in numbers is held to favour both the power of *concentration* and *distribution* according as the necessity of the moment may dictate; so that there is an elasticity in the employment of a force not attainable with a few large ships representing the same capital expenditure."

This was the case for smaller ships, outlined with scrupulous fairness by White, who then went on to demolish the argument by pointing out that in maintaining speed at sea and in steadiness of gun-platform, larger vessels were superior; they were less likely to be put out of action by a single blow, whether from gun, ram or torpedo; and carrying their powerful armament in one ship, under one direction, gave them greater power of concentrated attack; the fire of heavy guns in well-protected positions might be reserved until it was possible to deliver it with the maximum effect; and an action might well be fought with the secondary armament alone. Small ships could not carry heavy armour-piercing guns in well-protected positions, and destruction of unarmoured upper works was accomplished more rapidly when big guns were associated with quick firers.

On the question of the tactical advantages claimed for packs of smaller ships, White observed that many of the most experienced naval tacticians regarded the hypothetical *concerted attack* by several smaller vessels on a single large one as impossible in practice, while they ran serious risks of ramming or injuring each other during action.

"In fleet actions," he pointed out, "the corresponding risks would be even greater. Supposing seven or eight large ships opposed to 20 or 30 smaller ones; the difficulty of concerted attack, even in the earliest stages of an action, would be great, and it would become practically impossible later on. While the comparatively few large ships might act together and concentrate their attack on any selected portion of the flotilla of small ships, the corresponding concentration by a crowd of small ships would be impracticable . . . and the smaller ships would run great risks of being destroyed in detail by the larger."

This naval truth as expounded by White has been proved over the years.

But the Liberal government under Mr Gladstone were reluctant to increase expenditure on defence, although it was known that the French and Russian warship building programmes would put them on comparable terms with Britain by 1896. Faced with government inaction, the naval members – the Sea Lords – of the Board of Admiralty threatened to resign in a body if their advice to build more ships was rejected. The government gave in and found the money necessary for the proposed additions to the Fleet.

Included in the programme, to be spread over five years' building, were nine battleships of improved design – the *Majestic* class. These ships, of 14,900 tons, were a further increase in size over anything built previously, and a vindication of White's views as expressed in his memorandum to the Board.

The *Majestic* class, commenced in December 1893, were the finest examples of naval architecture in the world of their time. In the following eight years there would be 29 of virtually the same type built; a rare tribute to the quality of their designer.

White had the advantage of a new kind of armour, and a new wire-wound 12-inch gun, and both contributed to a saving in weight combined with greater efficiency. The barrels of wire-wound guns were made in stages and were much stronger than earlier designs. The main or inner barrel was made first and then bound round with layers of steel wire, the number of layers varying with the type and size of gun. The barrel was then encased in steel outer tubes with the wire remaining a hidden source of strength against the tremendous pressure generated for a split second inside the barrel as a giant shell was sent spinning from the mouth of the gun.

The *Majestic* class were armed with four 12-inch guns; twelve 6-inch; sixteen 12-pounders; twelve 3-pounders and five torpedo tubes. In elegance and efficiency they represent the peak of Victorian battleship design. White was to build other ships, but the *Royal Sovereign* and *Majestic* are those for which he is most remembered. A ship designer of genious, yet White was to end his great career on a poignant note.

In addition to his warships White also designed the new royal yacht,

Victoria and Albert. The ship was launched in 1899, but in July 1900 she heeled over in dock during completion. Although White had designed her perfectly, she had been overloaded with absurdly heavy fittings on and above the upper deck without White's knowledge, so that the report made to him after launching was unreliable in its estimate of weight to be added before completion. She had also been floated in dock with almost empty bunkers and water in only three boilers, a condition which increased her instability.

As Director of Naval Construction, White accepted full responsibility and received all the blame, although it was a subordinate who had had immediate supervision of the design and calculations. When the necessary adjustments of weight had been made the *Victoria and Albert* fulfilled every expectation in speed, seaworthiness and comfort and remained the royal yacht for 40 years.

But the shock to White, who had made his reputation with his original designs and calculations on stability (notably after the *Captain* disaster, when he devised improved methods of explaining the behaviour of ships at sea) resulted in a nervous breakdown.

He was violently criticized in Parliament and Press and although he carried on in office until January 1902, he exasperated his department during the last year by his lack of decision and constant worrying over trivialities: possibly the reaction of a man who had been once let down by a trusted subordinate.

His changed attitude lost him the loyalty of his staff; but even so, it is difficult to conceive the kind of cruelty to which they subjected him – probably in concert – on his last day at the office, 31 January 1902.

White sat alone in his room for some time and then went to where his senior assistants were at work.

"I am going now," he said. "Good-bye to you all."

No one spoke; no one rose from his seat. White glanced round the room, a pathetic figure, shunned at what might have been the time for a conventional sentimental ending to his brilliant career. He turned away and walked down the stairs alone. Only one man wished him well. His old messenger came forward and said: "May I shake your hand, Sir William, and say how sorry I am you are so ill as to be obliged to leave us."

During his retirement White travelled extensively in the USA and Canada, and often wrote for the Press on naval matters. He died on 27 February 1913.

The advance of the great ships went on; bigger and bigger, mightier and mightier. Science came ever more to the aid of gunnery, propulsion, communication and construction itself. But the technological progress of the 20th century at sea is outside the scope of this book. In fact, post-*Captain* development has been merely touched upon in this chapter, which covers only the most important ships from the point of view of design progress.

Just as Captain Coles might have marvelled at the *Majestic* class, so Sir William White would have been impressed by the size, power and technical complication of the capital ships he did not live to see and which, in their turn, became vulnerable to the technological advance of sea and air weaponry.

But it is interesting to reflect that the naval might of the 20th century felt its first embryonic pulse beat in the form of a gun on a raft, built by a naval officer with an inventive turn of mind as an improvisation in war.

It is thus that Captain Cowper Phipps Coles should be remembered.

APPENDIX 1
LIST OF SURVIVORS FROM
HMS *CAPTAIN*

		Age
James May	Gunner	36
James Ellis	Gunner's Mate	29
Lewis Werry	Captain of the Foretop	28
James Harvey	2nd Captain of the Foretop	29
George Bride	Coxwain of the pinnace	34
Charles Tregenna	Leading Seaman	26
John Heard	Able Seaman	24
Robert Herd	Able Seaman	24
William Lawrence	Able Seaman	20
David Dryburgh	Able Seaman	26
John Walker	Able Seaman	26
James Freeman	Ordinary Seaman	23
Henry Grange	Ordinary Seaman	20
Robert Tomlinson	Ordinary Seaman	19
Thomas Kernan	Ordinary Seaman	21
Francis Merryman	Boy 1st Class	18
James Saunders	Boy 1st Class	17
John Gribble	Boy 1st Class	17

Appendix 2

Nautical terms used in the book

sheet	sail-securing rope
halliard	sail-raising rope
mainsail	first sail up from deck
topsail	second sail
topgallant	third sail
royal	fourth sail

These sails may be on either the foremast, mainmast or mizzenmast on a three-masted ship, thus:

foretopsail	second sail up on the foremast
maintopsail	second sail up on the mainmast
brace	rope attached to yard for adjusting angle of sail to wind
yard	spar to which sails are secured
freeboard	height of ship's side above the water
bitts	large wooden posts with holes or slots through which sail control ropes were secured
reef	to reduce the area of a sail by rolling up and tying off part of it: sails may be single, double or treble reefed according to strength of wind

184

APPENDIX 3

GOVERNMENTS OF THE PERIOD

Party	Date	Prime Minister	First Lord of the Admiralty
Cons.	Feb. 1858–June 1859	Earl of Derby	Sir John Pakington
Lib.	June 1859–1865	Lord Palmerston	Duke of Somerset
Lib.	Oct. 1865–1866	Earl Russell (on death of Palmerston)	Duke of Somerset
Cons.	June 1866–1868	Earl of Derby	Sir John Pakington
Cons.	Feb. 1868	Benjamin Disraeli (on death of Derby)	Sir John Pakington
Lib.	Dec. 1868–1874	W. E. Gladstone	H. C. E. Childers G. J. Goschen

APPENDIX 4

POSTSCRIPT ... ANOTHER GENERATION

Gunner James May was a man of gentle and studious disposition who made his way up through the ranks from the lower deck to warrant officer in charge of gunnery. At the time when he survived the foundering of HMS *Captain* he had a 6½-year-old son, Thomas James, who was destined to spend his life in a variety of uniforms and to become a major in the Royal Field Artillery – and much more.

Major May, who died in October 1952 at the age of 88, spent much of his early life in South Africa in military formations, including the 3rd Mounted Rifles of the Bechuanaland Field Force, 1884–85; Victoria Rifles, Kimberley 1886; Diamond Fields Horse, 1889–95; Matabeleland Relief Force, 1896.

During the Boer War he commanded the Diamond Fields Artillery and was particularly associated with the conception and use of "Long Cecil", an impressive, breech-loading, field gun that fired a 28 lb shell. It stood about six feet high on wheels and looked like a regular piece of artillery: in effect, it was; but it had been made in the De Beers diamond mine workshop out of a billet of steel 10 ft × 10½ ins diameter, weighing 2800 lbs, part of the workshop stock. The gun was the idea of the mine's chief engineer, an American, George Labram, who built it. Long Cecil proved to be a formidable improvement on the seven-pounder guns that were all Major May had previously had with which to reply to the Boer siege guns.

May was mentioned in despatches twice during the war and from 1900–02 he became a District Commandant. He was made a Companion of the Order of St Michael and St George for his overall service in South Africa.

In 1914, at the age of 50, he transferred into the Royal Field Artillery and served in Europe throughout the First World War. Afterwards, he retained his connection with South Africa and was in charge of the educational, botanical and chemical section of the South Africa

186

Pavilion at the British Empire Exhibition, Wembley in 1924.

When World War II broke out Major May was aged 75 and from 1940–44 he served in the 12th Battalion, City of London Home Guard; and from 1942–43 he was finance officer for diamond control at the Ministry of Supply.

But this, apparently, was not enough for this remarkable son of an admirable father, who had spent virtually an average lifetime in British armed services. In 1944, at the age of 80, he managed to get himself transferred from the Home Guard into the Royal Navy. He served afloat for seven months in 1944 in an Emergency Crew, standing by with the Allied Fleet covering the D-Day landings and subsequent build-up in Normandy.

Major May was undoubtedly the oldest man serving at sea in the Royal Navy in 1944. He was asked if he had quietly shed a few years when he applied to serve in the navy and he replied: "No. I did not wangle my age on the form I had to fill up . . . I had no difficulty in getting leave from the 12th Battalion, City of London Home Guard to join the R.N."

It is quite possible that whoever dealt with Major May's application glanced through it without realising the significance of the year 1864; or else he or she was hopeless with figures.

However it may have been, Gunner James May would have been rightly proud of his son.

SOURCES

Captain Cowper Phipps Coles's correspondence with the Admiralty.
Captain Coles's letters to the Press.
James May, R.N., *Narrative on the Loss of HMS* Captain, Brompton, Kent, 1872.
O'Byrne's *Victoria Cross*, London 1880.
E. J. Reed, *Our Iron Clad Ships*, London 1869.
E. J. Reed, *A Treatise on Stability of Ships*, London 1885.
E. J. Reed obituary. Royal Institution of Naval Architects, London.
Proceedings of the Court Martial of Gunner James May, R.N. and others.
The Harrowby Manuscript Trust – The Ryder Papers. (By kind permission of the Earl of Harrowby)
Chronicle of the Murray Family by the Misses Murray, 1914. (Kindly supplied by Miss Kathleen Murray)
An account of the Whicher family. (Kindly supplied by Mr Peter Whicher)
The Gentleman's Magazine, November 1870.
The Times, miscellaneous reports 1860–70.
Hansard (Parliamentary Report) 1860–71.
E. K. Rawson, *Twenty Famous Naval Battles*, London 1900.
Sir John Dalrymple Hay, *Remarks on the loss of HMS* Captain, London, 1871.
Lieut-Colonel F. E. Whitton, *Service Trials and Tragedies*, London, 1930.
Admiral Ballard, *The Black Battlefleet – Mariner's Mirror*, 1931.
The Kentish Mercury, December 5th 1863.
Royal Navy Service records, Public Record Office.
The Diamond Fields Advertiser, Kimberley; and *South Africa*. (Research kindly carried out by the City of Kimberley Librarian)
Correspondence of Major T. J. May with the National Maritime Museum.
Miscellaneous press cuttings, Royal United Services Institute, London.
H. C. E. Childers, *Minute on the loss of HMS* Captain.
Sir Spencer Robinson's reply to the *Childers Minute*.
Admiralty correspondence and internal memoranda, 1860–70.
Sir Nathaniel Barnaby, *Naval Development of the Century*, London, 1904.
Dr Oscar Parkes, *British Battleships*, London, 1957.
Sir J. H. Briggs, *Naval Administrations 1872–1892*, London, 1897.
Dictionary of National Biography.

INDEX

189

Rice, Captain Edward, member of court
martial, 104, 105, 120, 125, 128, 139,
140
Rice, Lieutenant Ernest, evidence, 106,
107
righting lever, 73, 128
Robinson, Vice-Admiral Sir Spencer, 44,
56, 57, 67, 157, 160
relations with Childers, First Lord, 161
reply to Childers' Minute, 163
publishes correspondence with
Gladstone, 163–164
Robinson, Mr W. B., witness at court
martial, 115–118
Royal Albert, 25
Royal Carriage Department, 60
Royal Oak, 102, 178
Royal Sovereign, of 1637, 12
of mid-19th century, 40, 41, 45, 48
of late 19th century, 178
Royal United Services Institute, 26
Rumble, Mr, Chief Engineer, *Royal Albert*,
25
Russell, John Scott, 18
Russell, Lord John, Foreign Secretary, 59
Ryder, Rear-Admiral Alfred, 165, 168
Ryder, Edward, Midshipman, 102

St Paul's Cathedral, 170, 171
Saunders, James, Boy 1st Class, 90, 94
Scivens, lost after the sinking, 106
Scorpion, 59
Scullard, Mr, Portsmouth Dockyard, 43,
44
Seasalter, near Whitstable, Kent, 152
Shannon, 174
Sheepshanks, Commander, 80
Smith, Sir Frederick, M.P., 19
Smith, Alexander, Able Seaman, 102
Somerset, Duke of, First Lord of the
Admirality, 19, 27, 49, 51
Sebastopol, 24
stability, 70–76
Stewart, Rear-Admiral Sir Houston, 25
stokeholds, 88
Stanley, Very Rev. Arthur Penrhyn, Dean
of Westminster, 168–170
Stromboli, 24, 25
Swallow, 58
Symonds, Vice-Admiral Sir Thomas, 65,
67, 68

Taganrog, Sea of Azoff, 25
Taylor, W., Midshipman, 102
Thunderer, 174
The Times, support for Coles, 51, 153
Tomlinson, Robert, Ordinary Seaman,
90, 146
Trafalgar, 175
Tregenna, Charles, Leading Seaman, 86,
89, 90, 92, 93, 106, 143, 149
tripod masts, 69
Trusty, floating turret battery, 27
Turret Ship Committee, 44
Turret v Broadside test, 48–52
turrets, experimental, for coast defence on
Prince Albert, 28
cut down three-deckers, 40

US Navy Department, 31, 32

Vernon III, formerly *Warrior*, 28
Victoria Cross, instituted, 58
Victoria, Queen, 167
Victoria and Albert, 152, 181
Vigo, 67
Virginia State, 30
Virginia, 33
Volage, 65, 101
Vorster, Mrs Tini, 145

Warrior, first British iron battleship, 15,
20, 21, 28, 40, 42
Washington, 31
Watts, Isaac, 19, 125
Werry, Lewis, Petty Officer, 86, 91, 94,
106
witness at court martial, 149
Whicher, James, Deputy Inspector
General of the Fleet, 151
White, Sir William, 176–181
Whitworths of Manchester, 21
Wight, Isle of, Turret v Broadside test, 48
Coles's home, 60
Wivern, 58, 59
Woolley, Dr Joseph, 18
Woolwich, 60
Wrangler, 58
Wingate, W., Able Seaman, 102
Williams, Henry, Able Seaman, 102
Wise, Thomas, Able Seaman, 102

Yelverton, Vice-Admiral Sir Hastings, 67,
68, 81, 104, 105, 135, 137